Juliet's Letters from India

JULIET O'CONNOR
Copyright © 2018 Daniel O'Connor

Dedicated to Juliet and Dan's many friends throughout the years at St. Stephen's College, Delhi, and in particular to Alice and Satish Sircar for their unwavering kindness.

JULIET O'CONNOR

CONTENTS

ACKNOWLEGEMENTS

These letters were written exclusively by Juliet O'Connor, carefully preserved by her mother, Jessamine Wood, back in England and edited by her husband, Dan O'Connor. The process of publishing owes virtually everything to Phil Atkinson, who had already produced a new edition of Dan's mother's book, *A Far Off Bell*.

Juliet meets Nehru

Juliet's Letters from India 1963-72

Presented by Dan O'Connor

PREFACE

This is the story, in her own words, of Juliet, a young Englishwoman, and her life in India. A few short weeks after completing her college training in England as a teacher of art and crafts, she had her 21st birthday on August 10, 1963 and a week later married a young clergyman, Dan O'Connor. Three weeks later, they set sail for India, where they made their home, raised a family and lived until 1972.

With the end of the British Raj and the coming of Indian independence in 1947, it was unusual for people from the United Kingdom to settle for any length of time in India. A new cohort of experts of one sort and another did appear, but rarely stayed for more than months at a time. Only a very few continued to come and live in India, and most of these were missionaries. Among them were Juliet and Dan, recruited for work in Delhi, the capital. Both would be teachers, Juliet at Queen Mary's School and Dan at St. Stephen's College in the University of Delhi. They had waited until Juliet was through education college and they set sail in September. At this time. a sea voyage of about three weeks was still the normal way of getting to India, but only for a few years more. They were open to the idea of a long, even a lifelong stay, and were in India for a decade.

Apart from the introductory paragraphs, what follows consists almost entirely of extracts from Juliet's letters from India to her mother and father at their home (her birthplace) in the United Kingdom. She was a dutiful and loving daughter, writing home regularly, and—despite all her responsibilities and cares—reassured her parents by writing cheerfully and entertainingly.

Dan never saw Juliet's letters until after her death in 2016. He discovered them all neat and in order as her mother had preserved them.

* * * * *

I

Juliet wrote regularly to her parents at 37 Cranbourne Terrace, Stockton-on-Tees in the north of England. Her mother was secretary to a local company—Victoria Car Sales at nearby Yarm—and her father a freelance writer and artist, amateur astronomer and antiquarian bookseller. They were equally faithful correspondents, and though they must often have worried and wished us back in Britain, they very rarely said so, accepting our commitment to what we were doing. Those were difficult times for India, including two short wars with Pakistan and the struggle to build an independent economy and society, with a severe famine at one stage and frequent shortages and food-rationing. We were constantly hard-up, trying to maintain a hospitable home on very limited resources. Juliet's parents, far from well-off themselves, were incredibly generous in sending us parcels, food, clothes, magazines and newspapers.

Juliet was signed up by the mission agency as a teacher, provisionally at Queen Mary's, a girls' school in the Tis Hazari neighbourhood of Delhi, and I was recruited to be a lecturer in the English Department and chaplain of St. Stephen's, India's most prestigious university college.

India, when we arrived, was just sixteen years into independence, and under the brilliant visionary leadership of Jawaharlal Nehru, facing up to the immense challenges of an immense nation. In an earlier book *Interesting Times in India* (Penguin India 2005), I tried to describe our decade there in a more pedestrian and political memoir. Here, in Juliet's family letters, there is much more of what it felt like and how it impinged upon our life together and, when they arrived, upon our children. The city at that time had a population of just over three million, and its previous im-

3

perial occupants had given it a generous spaciousness, its planners putting New Delhi in 'a sea of foliage ...' We saw the beginnings of these changes while we lived there. Fifty years on, the polluted city of 10 million cars and approaching 30 million people leaves this the story of life in another world.

Our home was at the college. Founded in 1881 by a group of missionaries from Cambridge, it had soon become a leading institution in Delhi with a staff predominantly Indian teaching arts and sciences to university degree level and attracting ambitious young men, mostly Hindu, with some Christians, Muslims, Sikhs and others. Juliet often refers to them in her letters as 'boys' and indeed they started like English sixth-formers, a year or so younger than their British university counterparts. When we arrived, it was a college of some 600 students from all over India—all male at that time—some 250 in residence, many attracted by its high standards leading to careers in the Civil and Foreign services.

The staff was largely Indian, led sensitively with kindness and modesty by a Bengali, a former senior wrangler at Cambridge, Satish Sircar, alongside an English vice-principal, Ian Shankland. Alice Sircar became a very good friend to Juliet, and Elspeth Shankland, headmistress of the British School in New Delhi, soon recruited Juliet as a teacher, so that she taught part-time there and at Queen Mary's. Most of the college-staff wives had jobs about the city, so Juliet saw less of them than she would have liked. We were often joined by one or two young men, short-service graduates from Cambridge, but the college was essentially an Indian community. The chaplain, who was required to be a full-time teacher in one of the college departments, had always been an Anglican.

From 1940, the college had very attractive new buildings in the equally attractive setting of the former vice-regal estate. Other colleges and institutions of the University of Delhi arrived over the years as its neighbours. The college was laid out in four spacious residential courts centred upon the chapel and the teaching, social and administrative sectors, including the college hall where Juliet was to be much involved in student theatre. In the four courts glorious flowering trees and gardens tended by a small army of *malis* (gardeners) were a feature. Senior staff were housed about the college in the various courts. As previous chaplains had been unmarried and living in a set of rooms in one of these courts, it was necessary to build us a bungalow, though it was only completed and ready for occupation three months after our arrival. In fact, two new houses were built—providing us with good neighbours, the Aryas—on a site between the Allnutt Gate and an outer gate leading to University Road skirting the wild and wooded Ridge. A cluster of neem trees by our home attracted countless interesting birds. Though we were eager to live in this, the first home of our married life, it was fortunate that the house was ready for occupation only three months after our arrival, for that meant that during those early months we were gusts of the Sircars, with an opportunity to get to know them. They were kindness itself and lovingly helped us to settle to life in India.

When completed, our bungalow within its own garden on all four sides was attractively designed for a very hot country and had more angles than a traditional four-square house in order to catch whatever breeze or breath of air might be passing. When we moved in, we had a generous living-room opening onto a verandah, a dining room and kitchen, a study, two bedrooms opening onto another verandah, and two shower rooms. There was also a servant's room which, as we did not usually have a resident servant, we often used as a guest room.

Ten years in India were a life-shaping experience, with many wonderful features, and we loved our life and our home in this very attractive place, but there were snags. One was that I had been given two full-time jobs: first as a lecturer in English Literature with a full teaching load, and second as chaplain to a college community rising while we were there to approximately 1,000 students, only a small percentage of them Christian, though all—in our understanding—part of our parish. A very busy college life with consequent lack of time together was reinforced by the way the Bishop of Delhi frequently sent me to minister to congregations hundreds of miles out of Delhi. Juliet was rarely able to accompany me and had to endure a good deal of loneliness though she wonderfully established herself in the life of our college community.

An additional burden, especially for Juliet in managing our household, was the very poor pay that went with the job, much poorer than most mission agencies provided, and absurdly poorer than most expatriates. Juliet was only able to work for the first two years, until our first child arrived. My pay was fixed in 1963, and was soon much lower than that of our Indian colleagues with their increments. After being provided with travel tickets to get us to India initially, the Cambridge Mission expected us to find all subsequent travel to the U.K. out of our pay. Our final month's salary in April 1972, with children's allowances, came to Rs. 1,302.42, somewhat under £100. We immensely valued our parents' kindness in regularly sending us parcels of one sort or another to keep us going, but Juliet's intensely careful household management was our greatest asset.

A note about Juliet's style in her letters. She could write beautifully and to great effect, witness, for example, the limpid clarity and directness of the pieces included later, entitled 'Sisters' and 'Mushaira'. Her letters to her parents, however, were frequently something different. Those who remember those pre-email, pre-Skype and pre-iPhone days, will recall that a commonly used medium was the aerogramme, a strictly limited spread of paper on which one had to squeeze all the news. In family letters, then, Juliet developed a sort of shorthand and often dispensed with the niceties of complete sentences. Some of her more idiosyncratic abbreviations it has seemed advisable to replace with real words, while retaining generally the shorthand effect because that was how she wrote in her letters to 'Mama and Papa'.

A notebook of Juliet's, written much later, and hard to read because written when her hands were increasingly damaged by arthritis, refers to the weeks between our wedding and setting sail:

'Unlike many newly-married couples, we did not have a conventional start to our married life. Three weeks after our wedding day, we set sail for India. The intervening weeks were filled with a blissful but brief honeymoon in Edinburgh and on the Northumberland coast & frantic packing, including newly-acquired wedding presents. It seemed incredible that all our books and household equipment fitted into only seven tea chests. At the beginning of the packing fury, we doubted whether ten times seven would be adequate. Eventually, everything was safely packed, boxes labelled, and the carrier expected the next day. Unfortunately, the only junk room—and therefore suitable packing room —was at the top of my old home. This meant the manoeuvring of very heavy boxes down two flights of narrow and rather dark stairs. Husband and father spent an exhausting morning alternately scratching paintwork and collapsing into breathless panting heaps. When at last all the boxes were at ground level, they were joined by a crated refrigerator and an enormous crate containing our faithful second-hand Lambretta scooter. We certainly had misgivings about taking such things, but this was what we had been advised to take, and we were in no frame of mind to be deterred at this stage. We were, to say the least, fully expecting to have to pay excess baggage, but we were moving to the first home of our marriage, and even the addition of two trunks, and numerous suitcases could not damp our spirit at the last fence.

The following afternoon, the carrier arrived, and with effortless grace lifted our boxes into the waiting van. Our belongings all reached Delhi intact—and ten years later returned to Britain still intact.

Our departure day was preceded by a family gathering, with the addition of old friends, but the forthcoming attractions of what we envisaged as a holiday cruise tended to obscure something of the weight and importance of what we were doing. When the fated day arrived, however, we felt the increasing pressure of English time slipping away and a great unknown void rushing towards us. To call this a void is not completely true. It was more like a kaleidoscope in which fragments tumbled into view for a few seconds but in which nothing was really clear. Although not admitting to 'nerves', either to myself or to the assembled family, I was in fact violently ill and missed what I gather was a rather unenthusiastically eaten 'last' meal together. I was unconvinced of my own excitement, and actually felt no pangs of grief at the parting. With a few of our family and friends, we took the train from Stockton to Liverpool, staying overnight at a hotel close to the port.

"The ferry to Ireland?" asked the taxi driver as our family, pale-faced at the magnitude of our adventure, climbed into the taxi.

"No, the ship to India," we replied, hardly believing our own words. Friends followed in cars, and soon we were exchanging gifts and good wishes and counting cases on the dockside. Our mothers and friends seemed to cling to each other for reassurance as we strode confidently into the boarding shed where the final checking of our documents took place.

After very brief formalities, we boarded our vessel and climbed to a deck from which we could see friends and family below us on the quay. When they saw us there was frantic waving, but we had nearly an hour before leaving the dockside. This was no holiday cruise but the beginning of a frugal working life in a new country.'

[Her next notes, again, written much later, are hard to decipher beyond the opening] 'The journey was a glorious experience of sunshine and luxury.' The rest of our Indian story we must leave largely to her contemporary letters.

* * * * *

A JOURNEY OUT OF TIME

This was the title Juliet gave to her notes on the voyage to India, conveying something of a world that was—with the advent of air travel—soon to disappear.

The Anchor Line provided a passenger service between the United Kingdom and India, that is, between Liverpool and Bombay as it was then called, with three ships, the Cilicia, the Circassia and ours, the Caledonia, the latter carrying 320 passengers—all First Class—so that we all had the run of the entire ship. A young junior deck officer in the 1960s wrote of these as 'happy ships, well run and very informal and friendly, with a very Scottish feel'. That is how we found the Caledonia. Although including a number of Indian passengers, the Anchor Line ships were still regarded as the service used by the British '*burra sahibs*' and their ladies of the former empire. Enough of that feel was still around, hence Juliet's phrase, 'A Journey out of Time.'

The service to Bombay left Liverpool on Saturday, September 7, 1963 at 4 p.m. In that article, she wrote, 'Up on deck, we waved and exchanged strained stares with our well-wishers on the quay far below. The sound of the engines and the clanging of bells became more urgent as the ship cast off. We waved until we could no longer see them on the quay. Leaving behind the dramatic outline of the Royal Liver building, we slipped into the deep water of the main channel of the Mersey. Behind us, a city in miniature and all that was familiar, and in front of us a grey drizzle, the scent of the ocean, and the unknown. Only now did we realize the scale of our adventure'.

Juliet began to write her first letter to her parents on September 8. From that letter through to our final return to Britain in 1972, she was a most faithful correspondent with her parents—'Mama and Papa' as she always addressed them—writing regularly throughout the entire period. Both parents replied equally regularly.

* * * * *

Caledonia September 8, 1963

[Not yet into aerograms, Juliet added daily to this first, long letter until able to post it from Port Said in Egypt on the 16th]

Dear Mama & Papa,

It is very hard to know where to begin. There seem to be so many things to tell you, and yet I feel I must begin in Stockton & Liverpool. It was very hard to say goodbye to Daddy in Stockton & Mummy in Liverpool, but we both felt that through the sadness we had your blessing. You must look after each other during the next few years & this winter in particular. *[The previous winter had been very severe]*

Liverpool was really a most moving experience. We are still stunned. The actual moment of departure is hard to describe—really a fantastic mixture of feelings—not least our feelings for those left behind. Indeed, I think that was what was in our minds most, so please take care of yourselves.

Now I must try to remember all the fascinating details encountered so far.

Almost as soon as we set sail—in fact, still in sight of Liverpool, we had lifeboat drill. The cabin steward showed us how to put on our life jackets, & we all made our way to the allotted lifeboat stations. We were then read the regulations, & returned to our cabins.

Here is a plan of the cabin—much roomier than I expected.

[In a later piece, she added 'Our cabin was full of bouquets and telegrams, just like a 1930s film star's']

After a little unpacking, we had afternoon tea in the lounge. You hardly sit down before a waiter pounces with a tray of tea, etc.—marvellous. Here, we met Miss Gotch, a v charming old lady, very alive, jolly & sweet. She was returning to St. Stephen's Community in Delhi, where she had worked for many years. I was going to draw her for you, but she seems so nice that I won't because it might be hurtful to her.

After tea, we unpacked more, and then got ready for dinner—the first evening, one does not 'dress' for dinner. A fabulous meal. Fantastic choice of dishes, all beautifully cooked, perfectly served. Honestly, we are thoroughly pampered by the service—perfect. We have one table companion, 'J.G.Nicholls'. He has been in India 50 years, was first a tea planter, & is now an 'honorary game warden' in Assam. He is famous throughout the tea trade, so a tea planter here has just told us. Apparently he is very rich, and has just written a book called 'Fifty Years in the Wilds of Assam'. 'JG' talks all through the meal every meal, and is full of stories ranging from Anthony Eden in his golf club to men dismembered by bears! The waiter (one for each table—Indian) is v pleasant, & gives us an occasional sly look with regard to our table companion's constant chatter. It is all most pleasant.

Last night, the first, we watched quite a highish sea through the porthole, with the ship's lights reflected in the water. This morning, Sunday, we were wakened at 6.30 a.m. with orange juice, coffee and toast, brought by our cabin steward (Indian man). D had his shoes cleaned, then we went to Holy Communion at 7.15 a.m. This was held in the Gallery, a narrow lounge. There were perhaps 20-30 present, & it was v comforting.

Y'day, we booked our table, no.14, & we attend first sitting for all meals. This means breakfast 8.0, lunch 12.30, dinner 7.0, so this morning we finished church just nicely before breakfast, gorgeous breakfast menu, all beautifully served & rather delicious. Must break here to go to Community Hymn Singing in the lounge, which poor D has been roped in to help with.

Mon. Bay of Biscay—warm, bright sunshine, v blue sea.

The singing was alright, & we had a jolly chat and drink w. fellow travellers afterwards. After a few turns of the prom. deck, we retired about 11.30 p.m. The middle part of y'day was taken up by a morning service conducted by another clergyman & the Captain; and by v good food, reading & snoozing. The sea was quite rolling & swelling, & many are ill—but no effect on us (Hope I haven't spoken too soon!)

I can't tell you how pampered we are—its quite disgusting. There are stewards everywhere, all the time, & we have only to raise an eyebrow to have one ready to do our bidding. You will love this at the beginning of your holiday [*We had discussed the possibility of our two mothers in due time coming to visit us in Delhi*].

Y'day mid-morning, stewards were round the decks, public rooms &c. w. hot soup, and in the afternoon w. tea. We were in the smoke room for tea (with another clergy couple!), & we had not even sat down and there were four trays immediately put on our table.

This morning we had early orange juice, tea, etc., & then I had a shower whilst D slumbered. After a walk, we had yet another gorgeous meal, & are now to read in the sunshine.

Tues. off the coast of Portugal—past Lisbon. Bright & warm.

Firstly, let me try & remember y'day. Most of the time, so far, has been spent just lazing. We carry books always but soon fall to snoozing in the warmth and the comfort of those chairs. One couple with whom we are friendly come from Blyth in Northumberland (Methodist missionaries). The woman asked me soon after we met whether our wedding photograph had been in their Newcastle paper, 'The Journal'! We have also made friends with a charming major from the Indian army—just returning from a course on missiles; a couple of Indian girls, one of whom runs a nursery school in Bombay & is returning from a Montessori course; a tea planter and his wife; an oldish Indian couple who have been touring Europe—v well off and v friendly; and a couple from Outram Street, Stockton—an Indian married to an English girl. She, to put it bluntly, is a ghastly woman but they have my sympathy because of their difficulties in religion. He is Hindu.

The Chief Engineer has a place at our table in the dining room but appeared for the first time y'day lunchtime. We had Calcutta curry, which was delicious, but we were encouraged by him to have all the condiments—coconut, dried onion, raisins & mango chutney. He is a jolly Scot. The meals are wonderful but soporific.

After dinner last night, we talked w. the Stockton couple until 11.30 p.m.! I have v mixed feelings about the enjoyment of that! We chatted on deck until it grew too chilly—even in my mohair stole—& then retired to the smoke room for drinks & talk.

Y'day afternoon, have just remembered, we saw a P&O liner v close, bound for England. This was announced, and many hung over the side to wave. Also, have just remembered, I did some washing & ironing. This industry was perhaps rewarded by the fact that our waiter, noticing my partiality to the after-dinner mints, brought an extra-large dish-full, & after we had consumed a number at the table, without a word, wrapped the remainder in a paper napkin & handed them to me!

[In "A Journey Out Of Time" she wrote 'After dinner, as the air became hotter and heavier, it was pleasant to stroll beside the ship's rail, looking down at the bursts of phosphorescence in the sea and watch the churning foam smooth over and spread out in our wake. Above, the stars glittered like millions of diamonds in dark blue velvet. The reflection of the moon, a golden, rippling path across the sea, would have done justice to a Rita Hayworth film']

Back to y'day evening: coffee was brought round about 11 p.m., after which we retired. But just as D was preparing for bed, I decided it would be pleasant to have a walk. We therefore returned to the prom deck & walked. Is there, Papa, some sort of eclipse or similar, reckoned for last night —9th Sept. The moon was most peculiar, quite eerie. Partially obscured, & orange & v low from our viewpoint. This remained for about 20 minutes & then it was clear again & high. We finally retired & did not wake until the steward brought early tea. D went up on deck about 7.0 & dashed back down to summon me to see the sky—I've never risen so quickly in my life, but it was well worth it. Glorious reds, pinks, blues, gold, over an interesting bit of Portuguese coast.

The ship's course is plotted on a map, so we follow diligently. Places of interest are chalked on a board so we won't miss a thing! At the moment I can't see any coast ... we must be near 'Gib' ... should reach about midnight.

Really, there are some wonderful characters, including many 'my dear' people—ugh

Here is our food programme ... it really is disgusting ... lunch vast ... vast dinner ... We are collecting a full set of menus.

Tangier, 12.0

Wonderful Portuguese coastline this afternoon, with many fishing boats—have taken a few photographs. Can't describe how glorious it was. The Chief Engineer joined us again for lunch, & we had another curry, all v delicious. After a nap this afternoon, we looked at photographs of big game shoots, man-eating tigers & elephants from the collection of our table companion. It was fascinating, & then it was time for a shower before dinner. Have just thought, Mummy will probably read this while on the bus to your office at Yarm.

After dinner this evening, there was a dance—we listened to some of the music after watching a glorious sunset, & had a drink & a game of scrabble with the tea planter and his wife—charming people.

We are now cruising into the Med, with Tangier on one side and Gibraltar on the other. Unfortunately, all we know of this are the twinkling lights on both sides. Can we see the Milky Way here, Daddy?—think we have. The sky is fantastically full of stars—have never seen it so overfull before. Must to sleep as eyes are blinky.

Tangier, Wed.

Well and truly Africa. Holy Communion at 7.15 taken by D. Spent the morning sewing, & after a pleasant lunch, sat out in the sun and talked to a man who is an architect & is on his way to work on the building of a new provincial capital in Pakistan. The time slips by, and before you know what is happening, someone presents you with afternoon tea. Wonderful.

This evening, we had a film show, 'The Amorous Prawn'. A screen was tied to a mast, & chairs set out under the stars. At this part of the boat, there are coloured lights as it is used for dancing and general merry making. On such occasions, the stewards set out a long table with white cloths on the prom deck and the late coffee and sandwiches are served there. Tonight, it was incredibly warm at 11.0 p.m.—a soft, balmy breeze & the lights of Algiers in garlands and swirls not very far from us.

Today the fans have been in use & the air-conditioning in the dining room. We have the porthole open all the time & can see Africa just by sitting up in bed! The windows are wide open, & folks are discarding heavy clothes. Just can't believe that it can't help getting warmer & warmer. How I envy the Indian women. They wear the most gorgeous fabrics, chiffon, glitter and fabulous colours and get away with it!

Thurs. Tunis

This morn v near to the African coast. We can see houses and cultivated patches. The stewards are in all-white uniforms & v smart. White covers on the chairs. It is now 10.35 a.m. —30 mins. ahead of G.M.T. and ice cream has just been brought round, & in the distance I can hear the old familiar tinkle of coffee cups. What luxury. Am looking forward v much to your enjoyment of your outward journey, Mama. This ship is the best of this line, so you really must try & get a passage on this particular one. Everything is so clean and sparkling. Am in lounge with D. Shall now sew and await whatever anyone cares to bring me!

Fri. Malta/Tripoli

This morning to church, taken by Canon Timmins fr. Bombay—only 6 there with us and the celebrant. This morning & afternoon were occupied by sewing & reading & sunbathing. The early part of the afternoon is siesta time and there is hardly a soul on deck, but a little later we have a sunbathe before afternoon tea. Then it is sewing or reading or perhaps gentle exercise before a shower and dinner!

On Thurs evening there was 'Racing', a gambling dice game, but we did not go. Tonight, there was another film, 'Guns of Darkness'. This was rather gruelling but very good. Afterwards, we had the usual supper under the stars.

We saw round the kitchens this morning, and this afternoon visited the bridge—both v interesting but esp the bridge. This was all by public invitation—a general Open Day.

Sat. Tripoli/Crete

Before I forget, we have forgotten the Scrabble—it is in my cupboard downstairs. Could you please post it to us at St. Stephen's. We would find it very useful. Thank you so very much.

It is only 9.30 a.m. our time = 8 or 8.30 (can't remember which!) your time. Can just imagine you getting ready to go to work in sunny Saturday morning Yarm

This morning we received an invitation to cocktails with the Captain! So this evening we shall don our gladrags & get with it!
We are in the lounge and D is writing up on Bishop Cosin [some research work], so I shall now read and sew.

Sun. 15, Alexandria

This hasty, just before lunch, so you will have to wait for the next instalment to hear about the Captain's cocktail party.

It is jolly hot but delicious.

Take care of yourselves.
God bless.
Fondest love.
Juliet

Caledonia Sun.

[the first aerogramme]… a brief letter—there is a longer one in the post, but, because it is so bulky, it is sent by a different system. It is in the form of a diary, so nothing has been missed.

Now it is gloriously HOT, and the baggage room is like hell! We've packed away our heavy clothes and just snooze in the heat of the Med. Honestly, I've never seen a blue sea like it—fantastic. I've told you in the big letter just how pampered we are … For your sake, and the thrill of the journey, I hope you come to see us.

Have worn that new dress successfully for dinner—a diff one every evening so far!

September 17, 1963. Suez Canal

… the Captain's cocktail party started at 7.15 p.m. and we were introduced by the chief dining-room steward (sort of toastmaster person) to Captain John Gibson O.B.E. He mentioned Paddy's uncle to us, & was v genial … After choosing our drinks, we found two old stagers of the Raj days to talk with … such an exclusive gathering! … about 20 at the most.

[In "A Journey Out Of Time" Juliet adds, Many of the passengers were rather elderly women who might, perhaps a little unkindly, be called remnants of the Raj. These ladies were often conspicuous by their braying voices and their wrinkled, leathery skins, despite the large hats they wore in the sun, and the slightly old-fashioned, sensible clothes, but above all for the particular tone of voice they used when addressing non-white members of the crew. They rarely looked straight at the stewards, unless angry, and gave orders in a confident, off-hand manner]

One of the women we talked with is the wife of Oscar Brown, the last British judge in Bombay. Simply <u>everyone</u>

knows Oscar, darling! Another woman lives in India with great glee because she says that at her age (40-ish) in England one has to settle down to 'being a Mum', whereas in India she can go out in shorts to badminton and do all sorts of younger, interesting things! Another woman, a widow, has travelled on the Caledonia 4 times in the last 8 months! Apparently her husband left money in India when he died (they had lived there practically all their lives) & as you can't bring money out of India, she keeps holidaying there to use it up! Our '50 years in Assam' man was there, a few Indians and a few more Europeans. All rather charming! The party finished at 8 in time for dinner. The widow woman thinks she will come and visit us in Delhi—as do so many others!

Tues. The Red (hot) Sea

When we arrived at Port Said, about 11.30 p.m.on Sunday, immediately we were surrounded by little boats crammed full of leather pouffes, cases, bags, all sorts of basketwork, oriental slippers, knick-knacks, toys, hats, jewellery, carpets … v colourful indeed. In each boat were two men, one to row, the other to sell. The selling partners shouted to the passengers hanging over the side of the ship, such phrases as 'You buy lovely carpet ….Hey, you, white girl, you catch me rope—very cheap, half price'… goods & money were exchanged by lowering a rope. Here is one example of bargaining: an Egyptian wanted £3-10-0 for one pouffe, and in the end sold it for 10/-! Egyptian customs men came on board to check the passports of those going ashore—some of the more foolhardy—not us! Some of the merchants also came on board … one changing money, offering 16 rupees to £1 (normal 13) … The buying and furious bargaining went on for several hours—we retired at 2 a.m. We were very tired but wouldn't have missed it for anything.

Just remembered that in the Med, just before Port Said, we watched flying fish—hundreds of them. It is fantastic how fast they fly and how far. Beautifully graceful. We also watched a couple of porpoise playing just under the bows. They leapt and frolicked in glee.

Before I talk of the actual canal, I must just say that indoors y'day it was 91F. Today, it is fantastically hot—just pouring w sweat—but we understand that it is not so hot in India—even the Goanese stewards are feeling a little warm. The Red Sea is supposed to be the hottest place in the world, because of the deserts on either side.

Now to tales of the canal: Here is a list of what we saw:- ... a man ploughing w two oxen, a pitifully poor farmstead w shacks & a few stooks of corn drying. Loaded donkeys and men in 'nightshirts' & women walking behind in long black dresses—from head to foot. Three men dressed in black with 'Lawrence of Arabia' headgear, riding into the desert on camels ... A train with crowds of people on the roof. Gt hawk-like birds of the desert.

The pilot who takes us through the canal brought his little boat onto our foredeck, & his two companions slept on the hatch covers. During the day, one of them rigged up an awning and opened shop! —sandals, hats, trinkets.

We saw lots of tankers going through the canal & a few Egyptian traders. As far as scenery could be seen, miles of desert stretching as far as the eye could see. We were tied up in a siding for 7 hrs. & the sun & reflection off the sand were unbearable—or so we thought until we reached the

Red Sea. Ships going south always have to tie up to let north-bound traffic through the canal. This is so the full oil tankers do not have to stop—to avoid accidents.

Now in the Red Sea we feel like lumps of toffee, wet & sticky all the time. Had 3 showers y'day and it makes not the slightest difference. Temp in the 90s and we shiver in our air-conditioned dining saloon where it is down to 78! Sounds unbelievable. We could bear the heat if it wasn't humid.

Tomorrow (Fri.) we are to shop in Aden—our first dry land since we sailed.

Almost forgot—the Gulli Gulli man! He is a conjuror who sails down and up the canal, performing on each liner. He produces chickens from people's shirts and under tins. Also does illusions with little bricks, and throws borrowed money away, & then it is found in someone else's pocket! A v good children's show which astounds the kids, and a 'Grand Show' for adults in the evening. He keeps repeating "No chicken, no rabbit, no mongoose, hocus pocus mallocus, gulli gulli gulli"—v good & v funny.

Last night there was a fancy dress dance and a fish & chips supper in paper! There has also been more racing. This morning (Thurs) we got up early and were in the pool at 6.0 a.m.! Gorgeous, & we had it to ourselves.

Must post this today and write some others. Suggest you read this in part to Nana and Poppa [Js grandparents]. Take care of yourselves. God bless. Fondest love. Juliet. & love from D.

Indian Ocean, Sept. 23, 1963

[First paragraph typewritten] This is our prize from Aden. I can not remember where the last letter finished, so I shall begin in Aden. We arrived early on Friday morning, which is a Muslim Sabbath or somesuch, so some of the shops were closed. After waiting around for ages whilst the officials negotiated, we were taken by small boats to the mainland. Someone on the ship had told us of a reliable shop in Aden for such purchases as this typewriter, so we made straight for it. As you know, it is a duty-free port, so there are vast differences in prices for almost everything. There were many makes of typewriter, and we chose this Japanese one at £12! It really is a little beauty.

Have just had coffee, and will now continue, but in biro … On first arriving in Aden, we were pestered by taxi drivers who wanted to take us to the 'Real Aden'—ie the old city. Others pestered us to buy jewellery, etc—pester, pester, pester. That was the really awful thing about it. Here is a list of what we saw: goats roaming the streets, lots & lots of them. Everyone in national dress, which meant the women in purdah—fantastic! Beggars in the street. A blind man being led by a little girl/boy?—really biblical. Fruit and such on sort of litters. Very narrow streets crammed with higgledy piggledy open-fronted shops. There were a few Chinese shoe-makers with a great range of wares. We took photographs, so you will see for yourselves!

We met some friends and went into a low Arab dive for a Coke—safe because it was bottled. The sun was really blazing, delicious after the ghastly humidity of the Red Sea. Some people were asleep in the streets. I bought some new sandals (made in Italy) from a Bata agency.

The landscape around Aden is fantastically barren with great pinnacles of rock in most delightful fairy-tale shapes.

We returned to the ship for lunch, but afterwards, D went ashore again. We'd had your letters, with news of a very healthy tax rebate, so we cd afford some binoculars that D had rather coveted. Japanese again, only £3.10. They are v small and slip into a pocket. On the same trip, D bought some scent as a prize for me!

During the whole of the day there were little boats selling all sorts of wares—they pestered, but not half so bad as Port Said. The bargaining is fascinating but horrible to hear. I'm longing for you to see the photographs—we got another film in Aden, costing only 23/- instead of 36/-.

Saturday night was film night. 'The Wrong Arm of the Law', Peter Sellers. We also saw a Hayley Mills film—quite film fans! Last night we went to a performance put on by passengers, quite entertaining—instead of Community Hymn Singing!

This morning, HC at 7.15 a.m. and Morning Service at 10.30 a.m. Quite a pleasant if not v active day. We had cocktails with the Chief Engineer before dinner—v select, only 6 guests !!!—a mad social whirl we are living in!

Next stop Karachi, and we are going ashore, so are looking forward to it. I find it rather cold today—hope it improves.

Tues.

We can see Karachi in the distance—doesn't it take a long time to get to India! I can't wait to reach Delhi, but will be sorry to lose some good friends we have made. Fortunately, one of the best, the army major, is resident in Delhi at least for a time.

Last night was Gala Night—paper decorations, hats, flags, special dinner, dance, etc. I don't think we really caught the spirit of things—seemed a little too contrived & we are hardly the dancing till dawn type ! I can hear you calling us stuffy!. This seems a v short epistle in comparison w former such, but soon we disembark, and that change of activity should provide plenty of readable material.

So pleased the flowers pleased. Take care, God bless. Fondest love. Juliet.
So delighted by the separate letters—keep it up!

[Letter missing, but Juliet's "A Journey Out Of Time" concludes, 'At long last, when we went up on deck after breakfast, there was a slight spicy edge to the air, and in the sea we saw great earthen brown streaks from the rivers of India sweeping down from the distant Himalayas and over the broad plains carrying the precious earth out into the ocean. It seemed as if India was coming to meet us, and, as we said farewell to our fellow travellers, we began to feel the warm welcome of our new country enfolding us in its magic'.]

Mission House, Bombay. 28 Sept. 1963

You must excuse this short epistle, but our travelling prevents much more … I'll bring you up to date in greater detail later.

On Wed.morning we had a tour of Karachi (Pakistan). There were 2 car loads & it was FANTASTIC! We rocketed from lush embassies to wicker shacks on the sidewalk. We saw camel -, donkey-, bull- and horse-drawn carts; water carriers, shavers on the sidewalk, ear-cleaners, beggars, lots of new buildings, & miles & miles of squalid bazaars, and visited a museum (armed guard with fixed bayonet!) ... & 2 shrines, where we removed shoes—one of the latter was alive with eariwigs and cockroaches, ugh.

Friday, we arrived in Bombay—just cannot believe it. All our boxes intact ... nothing missing.

We are comfortable, and a friend from West Hartlepool met us and took us home for lunch, round Bombay and to a gorgeous swimming pool ('Europeans Only' after 16 years of independence!)

Rather hot and sticky in Bombay—have tasted first guavas and do not like them. Just finished last Smarties *[J's favourite English sweets]*.

Bombay is also fantastic, but I just accept what I find, and like what I find except for human degradation. We have bought supplies for the train journey, & set off at 7.30 p.m.

It is fantastic, the amount of street noise all night, and the birds singing too. First night under a mosquito net & I hadn't a clue where I was this morn.

It is now just about siesta time, but in England you will just have settled down to work, about 9.20. That also seems absurd.

Have been called memsahib a few times.

Bought from the Mission House some gorgeous, v fine crochet work, 19-piece dinner set

Take care. God bless. Fondest love & love from Danny. Juliet.

* * * * *

1963 DELHI

St. Stephen's College, Delhi Oct. 1, 1963

Thank you for yr delightful letters

Well, just can't believe we are actually HERE, DELHI. Dark again when the train arrived, but we had a wonderful welcome at the railway station from Sircars, Shanklands, Rajpals & Miss Froggatt. Now we are with Sircars and v comfortable—every convenience (inc. servants!). [Alice & S.C.Sircar—principal; Elspeth & R.I.Shankland—vice-principal, Lotte & W.S Rajpal—dean, Clare Froggatt—head of St Stephen's Community]

The actual Frontier Mail train journey was wonderful, v exciting & wonderful air conditioned carriage w every convenience *[our first and last air-conditioned train journey]*

On the way to Delhi we saw exotic birds, greens & reds etc, and cranes and similar birds. Also camels, and water buffalo wallowing in muddy rivers & shack villages & temples & mosques & a motley crowd of people.

The day we left Bombay, we spent shopping in the bazaars, & it was all one hears of such places—wonderful, and no pestering like in Pt Said & Aden.

(This is a v jumbly letter, but you can imagine we are v excited!). The day we left Bombay was the first of a 3-day festival & everyone was wearing flowers; even cars and sewing machines at tailors' shops were decked out. On the pavements stylized flowers were drawn in chalk.

Now to the Sircars & Delhi (we will live in their guest suite until our house is ready). Their house & garden are lovely … in the latter wild peacocks (with a noise like cats), partridges, rabbits, pigeons and gorgeous butterflies. Squirrels play in the garden & come onto the verandah. There are also lizards, & at night they hang on the verandah ceiling, round the light, waiting for insects. In the actual Univ grounds there are cattle wandering about. There are, of course, plenty of ants & a few beetles!

This really is the most fabulous & sheltered place—can hardly believe we are in a huge city.

The college chapel is beautiful—white & v simple & lovely—we will be sending slides of these places.

Our house is not yet finished but we have photographed the progress so far. I am rather useless at the moment because it is impossible to unpack any of the chests … Just can't wait to get going.

College has now finished for a 2 wk break, so we were in time to see it working, then D has 2 wks to get organised. Only wish the house was ready.

Y'day we were shown round College, and tonight there is a big Coll. dinner, & tomorrow evening we are to dinner w the Shanklands.

The transport in Delhi is v varied: buses, horse-drawn tongas, scooter rickshaws, taxis, bullock carts, donkey carts, camel carts, bikes, scooters, cars. It sounds and looks a nightmare.

Take care. God bless. Juliet & Danny

St. Stephen's Coll, Delhi, Oct 7, 1963

It is so nice to get 2 letters. ... On Friday, we went out to dinner & had a delicious meal ... by candlelight ... in the garden w the crickets singing and a full moon v silver in a deep dark. blue tropical sky ... the evening was perfect ... after it, we all went for a drive round Delhi ... including the magnificent Secretariat building in New Delhi. We also had a look at the British, Russian & magnif. American embassies ... like palaces, esp. the last. All over the broad lawns in the Sec. area people were having moonlight picnics—it was wonderful.

On Sat. morn we visited, w. Mr Sircar, who is v keen to show us everything, the Red Fort ... a magnificent building ... the most glorious painted walls & ceilings & mosaic floors, impossible to do justice to in a letter. When we looked from a balcony, men w performing bears & monkeys came and pranced about ... also went to a huge mosque, I think supposed to be the largest in the world. Also bought fm. Delhi Cloth Mills khaki material for D's cassocks.

Had letter from Janet *[English college friend]*

We are looking fwd. to our garden, esp grapefruit as there is a tree already there. House is continuing—we inspect every day, so they have got to keep on working! We have now found a cook-bearer called Babu Lal & so now only require a part-time sweeper. Just can't wait to move into the house.

One evening (the day after Gandhiji's birthday) we had a run out to his shrine (removing shoes, as in mosque). On his birthday, many important people went to circle his shrine! Pandit Nehru was there, but we missed him.

We have seen gt. flocks of green parrots, , vultures—and peacocks flying in the tops of trees. We also saw jackals, and heard their ghastly calls, just across the road, on the Ridge.

Also the other evening, we went to a village—quite indescribable, but will attempt to in next letter.

The mail has just arrived, posted 4th Oct., this is 7th, so that is quick. Thank you Papa for the 'typical Sunday morn. letter'. Today … a typically hot afternoon, & soon is siesta time. Remembered that today is your wedding anniversary, so happy anniv from us both. Do you realise that we have been married for 7 whole wks!

We are having a film processed, so the first slides shdnt be so long arriving in England.

Take care, fondest love. God bless. Juliet.

St. Stephen's College, Tues. Oct 15, 1963

Well—the temperature continues over 100—doesn't seem possible, does it? At night it is cold at 70 and I wear a woollen! Can just imagine you over the fire at 37, but can't imagine the coldness … wrap up carefully. Hope you will go to Janet's wedding, Mama.

I promised to tell you about the village we visited. It was 'gathering gloom'. Night comes quickly here, and we arrived half way between day & night. A muddy, dusty track led through the village, w. thatched mud huts on either side

& tatty blankets over some of the doorways ... the utmost squalor: crumbling dwellings crowded together & cattle all over the place. Lots of people & children everywhere, too. A few huts had lights, & cooking cd be seen in progress. There were women coming from the well with waterpots on their heads ... slightly eerie because of the darkness. At the far end of the village was a Hindu temple, and we cd hear the rhythmic clanging of different bells ... Inside, it was dimly lit, but we saw a goddess on a raised dais. About 12 people inside were ringing bells together—not much prayer about it—children wandered in and out—all v casual—fine stuff for a novel about the mysteries of India—it couldn't have been more primitive.

We have also been shopping, and bought a delightful work-basket & crockery & kitchen utensils & curtaining. I am now busy making curtains—the Principal also enjoys sewing, and so he made the study ones!

One morning we stopped in the middle of Delhi for a huge herd of water buffalo to pass, & we were forever avoiding cows.

This is rather disjointed but must try & mention everything. During a walk on the Ridge, we saw a flock of about 40 parrots flying round & round ... hoopoes, & brilliant blue & green birds. Vultures. Jackals come into the Prin's garden every night after his 4 geese—but they are always safely locked away!

The other night we listened to Arthur Haynes on the radio!

Please will you send me the BERO Cookery Book, Mama.

We have been to our first garden fete—delightful. We bought some candlesticks and some silvery leaves for Christmas. Have also been to the blessing of a new school. These things are all terribly, terribly nice (as you can imagine!).

Tonight we are out to dinner. Mrs. Sircar takes us to visit people almost every day. I really think she has adopted me! We went to a birthday party tea the other day.

Tomorrow I visit Queen Mary's School, where I will be teaching. On Friday, we go to St. Stephen's Hospital for St. Luke's Day celebrations, and on Sunday we go to a church dinner to celebrate their 96th anniversary. Coll. starts again tomorrow, and poor D is rushed off his feet.

... soon, we'll be sending you a parcel, a Caledonia/India miscellany ... As I write, you will just be rising

Delhi, Oct. 22, 1963

We are thinking of you all at St. Peter's, but it seems like something in outer space. Can just imagine little Yarm in the October sunshine, and the gypsy fair about now.

We now have a fuse box in our house, but we need mains connection, bathroom fittings, windows, locks ... Sircars are sweet and hospitable, but we are longing to unpack our boxes.

Queen Mary's School ... I have been offered a wonderful job, age group 5-8+ but have <u>my own art department</u>! I will be in complete charge. There might also be some English lit. in the higher school ... hours to suit me, mornings only ... start after Christmas, all looks rosy. Other offer at the British School—all subjects, 6 year old, but am not interested really.

St. Luke's celebration—tea and a service on the hospital lawn, all rather charming & terribly nice—meeting all the notables.

Oct 19. Shopping and pricing furniture—all terribly cheap.

Oct 20 - 96th Anniversary of church, St Stephen & the Delhi Martyrs—we were 'special guests'— one of the most wonderful Evensongs I have ever been to—in Hindustani— we sang it under our breath in Eng! Church packed, and gosh, cd they sing! ... afterwards, a church feast under the stars in the middle of Delhi ... pillau, curry (v v hot) & sweet rice. At the moment ... Dasserah , a Hindu festival ... drama, play-acting of the myths—the exile of Ram and all the rest of it! In the midst of all this, our hymn-singing witness was tremendous.

D has a service every morning in chapel, and I go with him to evensong.

29 Oct Queen Mary's School speech day—Chester Bowles, US Ambassador, the speaker .... Jangpura School Fete

When we arrived at Bombay, I got weighed—9st 6lbs ... y'day 7st 12 lbs—isn't it absurd! Yes, the scales are reputable!

St. Stephen's College, Oct. 30, 1963

Gosh, I seem to have been so busy lately, but here at last is a letter.

The house is not quite ready yet, but we now have glass, bolts and paint !! ... perhaps in a week.

This week ... supply teaching at the British School, Eng, Hist and Maths—so on Friday we are going to buy a 3-piece suite with my wages! For the British School, I have a driver each way and a CD car, leaving home at 7.30 a.m

The other afternoon, I went out to tea in New Delhi, & my friend sent a car for me—driver in smart white uniform! (Boy, am I lapping it up!)

Last Sunday, D took early service at St Thomas Church, and we stayed for b'fast with the principal of the school.

Chapel numbers are increasing, and we are happy with progress so far. D is working v hard. Doubly so because he hasn't yet got the books he needs out of the tea-chests

We had a wonderful lampshade buying expedition the other morning and came back laden. The morning ended with pink ice cream and hot chocolate in the proper manner!

Every day, I feed the birds on the lawn, &, apart from sparrows (who hang about at 4.30 p.m.) I had 10 jungle warblers, 3 mynas, 2 doves, a hoopoe and 5 squirrels. The sparrows sleep on a ledge in the bathroom each night ... Also a skinny lizzy. We also have a mouse in the dressing room.

No sign of the scooter yet, just more and more forms to fill in.

Friday evening, we went out for dinner, & Saturday another sale of work/fete

D dines in coll on Wednesdays

St. Stephen's College, Nov. 14 1963

Can't imagine your bitter cold temperature—here the range is 50-90—I often wear a sweater all day!! D can't bear the heat!

Still supply teaching because the house is not ready.

British School—I am in fact earning the most I possibly could in Delhi and will get less at Queen Mary's. I have to go right across the city every morning—over the Ridge, along the Jumna, past waterholes with wallowing buffalos, down Rajpath and past the President's house—all by CD car! ... lunch with my English friends, the Workmans, steak & chips, and soufflé.

D &I have had 3 v pleasant shopping expeditions ... kitchen things packed into a bucket .... Furniture, a 3-piece wood and cane affair ... We now have a favourite restaurant in Connaught Place for ice cream, cream cakes and tea ... home by scooter rickshaw in the dark, twinkling lights around—lovely silhouettes of mosques against the evening sky. The third trip was to insure the scooter, which has now arrived.

We eat a mixture of Indian & English food, and know a couple of safe eating places in New Delhi. I like going to Cottage Industries to look at the tourists!

More & more flowers are blooming now.

We need water and electricity, and grills on the windows, and then we can move in.

This morning we went out to coffee with the Cantwell Smiths—Wilfred teaches comparative religion, and is going to Harvard in the spring.

Three visitors for coffee at the Principal's—v woolly about their reasons for a round the world trip ... on the cadge ... I was outraged about their waste of the Prin's time.

Have seen several mongooses/mongeese? in the garden, and a big monkey.

D went to Jaipur to take a service last weekend, so was on my own, & the jackals were particularly bad—the howling of hunting packs is ghastly—there is no other word for it.

Saw some brilliant green budgie-type birds this morn. Last night, we wondered why the curtain was moving, and found our resident mouse half way up.

Delhi, Nov. 2, 1963

Thank you so much for so many letters, and for such a wonderful art book, Papa.

The death of Kennedy—we are stunned by all the horror of it.

... not in the house yet! It is now quite cold night and morn, & I shd like my warm clothes from the boxes. We've had a terrific thunder & lightning storm, and today it poured with rain—absolutely drenching.

Am delighted and overjoyed by the prospect of 'Housewife' magazine. Also could you buy and send a Good Housekeeping-type diary—the sort with household account spaces.

... it was v interesting to see the Teesside Gazettes.

Have had Christmas cards from Auntie Reta, Nana & Poppa and the Bp of Durham, so far.

Saw 2 elephants and a camel caravan y'day. Am just longing to show Delhi to you.Mama.- hope you are saving hard—believe me, its worth saving for. Its absolutely wonderful—all the flowering trees and flowers are out now & the place is gorgeous.

The scooter is registered & we have joined the AA of Upper India.

Am in touch with Janet & Sylvia [another college friend].

Tomorrow night, we are going to coll performance of 'Twelfth Night'—so shall wear black dress 1 ... hair-style changes—am growing it [drawings provided].

D is working v hard & seems a bit tired & ready for a holiday. We feel all will be well when we move into our own home.

Take care of yourselves in that ice and cold.

St. Stephen's College Dec. 8, 1963

… I'm wearing 3 sweaters and I'm still frozen—my feet are like ice. D loves the 'freshness' but I'm just miserable … middle of the day is not so bad, but dark mornings and freezing nights are ghastly. D's head is brown, but I'm just my old colour.

Still not in the house—we need occupation cert. & grills on the windows.

Am busy setting school exam papers.

Y'day was Founders Day … student variety show, v rowdy & funny—takes one back!

… bought a brass candlestick for our Christmas candle. We are both going to hang up our stockings!

I sometimes see elephants on my way home from school. Saw some saffron-robed monks w begging bowls. Am sure you wd find all this fascinating. Save for all you are worth—even sell the sideboard, because you must come!

Dec. 13, 1963 The British School, New Delhi

Thank you so much for the wonderful Christmas cake ... also for Scrabble. It is lovely to have a parcel, but most unfortunate to have to pay through the nose to customs to get it.

The gate-posts are built, but the people who really matter, the contractors, are just lazy crooks.

We had an earthquake, & I slept through it ... another tremendous thunder storm.

Coming from chapel last night, a couple of jackals ran through the hedge.

PS—just back from the reception. We have actually been presented to and shaken hands with the Prime Minister, NEHRU! How about that! .... only ten weeks after reaching India ... invited by Violet Alva, Deputy Speaker of the Upper House—everyone was there, cabinet ministers, ambassadors, bishops, and US—we shall send photographs of our presentation—hope you keep the family informed of such happenings!

Delhi, Dec. 18, 1963

This is an attempt to get a letter to you as close as possible to Christmas Day.

D has been asked to help at the midnight at St. James Church within the Kashmere Gate

On Christmas Day, we shall think of St. Peter's and 37 and 52 *[grandparents]* There is not a hope of being in the house for Christmas … a wonderful college carol service … we decorated chapel and had a crib … lots and lots attended, not all Christians either. D gave a good address.

Hope all is well and cosy at 37 for Christmas. God bless. All our love. Juliet & Danny.

Christmas Day 1963

Just finished breakfast after 8 a.m. communion. D helped at midnight at St. James, which was broadcast on All India Radio (I listened in), and has gone off to help at Urdu service in New Delhi

On 21st, Christmas shopping … we had a v cosy lunch in our usual restaurant … a v happy day. Lots of shops in N Delhi have Christmas things & there are trees & holly & mistletoe …. Can imagine little Yarm and Stockton at Christmas & the awful packed shops—e.g. Boots upstairs!

On 23rd, we went to take communion to a gathering of Christians at Hissar, about 100 miles from Delhi, 4½ hours by bus. The bus itself was an experience and of course we were the only 'pinks'. A member of the congregation put us up, and we were back in Delhi at 5 p.m. on Christmas Eve. The villages were fascinating … wonderful, noble-looking people, naked children, monkeys, camels, mule trains, oil wells, miles of desert scrubland. We carried our bedding rolls for our journey into The Punjab!

In the evening, the Shanklands wined and dined us by the fire, with carols on the radio—all v delicious and v kind.

We are not in the house, so are keeping the cake to celebrate when we get in.

Brrr freezing—a friend has loaned me some winter skirts so I can survive.

Lunch today will be in the Sircars' huge garden. Our garden is also huge—including veg plot. You will love it when you see it—keep saving!—we accept no excuses.

We seem to have collected another round of invitations ... am longing to be able to have people back to our home.

Babu Lal is acting as bearer for us at Sircars' ... he brought us garlands this morning for Christmas, and the gardeners brought us buttonholes, and the dhobi [laundryman] garlands—and after church we all got buttonholes. D has given me a gorgeous red velvet-lined jewel box ... going out to tea this afternoon.

Give our love to everyone.

* * * * *

1964 OUR INDIAN HOME

'Home' Jan. 1, 1964

At long last, we have moved in. At least, we slept here on New Year's Eve, but we are still eating at Sircars.

Our furniture is here, and we are unpacking the tea chests—hardly any casualties. We are working like fury—today we have almost set the kitchen to rights, including gorgeous, gorgeous fridge [wedding present from Juliet's parents] …. We just can't believe such lovely things in such a wonderful house can really be ours.

The cook is delighted with the kitchen, and is proud to show people round. We have also organised bread man, egg man, milk man, newspaper man

You see, I've suddenly turned into a housewife !!

'Home - The Study' Jan. 5, 1964

Our cook is a gem—everything is perfect, gorgeously flavourful … I just order and leave it to him—fabulous … The cook calls me Madam (very apt, I think!) & Danny the Master. Sweeper boy, a v willing worker, calls us Memsahib and Sahib or Padre Sahib.

Here is a sort of tour of the house [plans of each room and its contents, drawings of lampshades etc … colours of curtains]

Starting school at the end of the month.

Diary : giving tea party Monday and Wednesday, dinner party Wednesday, out to dinner party Thursday.

'Home' Jan. 9, 1964

Here is a more detailed conducted tour *[more detailed plans]*

The cook, Babu Lal, is a gem. Everything he cooks is perfect. All I have to do is issue fridge stuff, and order the meal and write a shopping list ... Our first dinner party last night went very smoothly ... began w a delicious soup. He makes delicious soup every night, seemingly out of nothing. After stuffed tomatoes and cauliflower in white sauce, a chilled chocolate soufflé with cream (we get masses of cream every day from the buffalo milk). As we finished cheese & biscs, he took coffee into the sitting room so all was ready there ... I can rely on him utterly. He lives w. us.

College gardeners bring flowers and arrange them in vases that I provide ... sweet peas, nasturtiums and pansies this week. The barber calls & cuts D's hair, and wd manicure my nails if I wanted. The dhobi collects washing! Missionaries! But we do feed others, and look after the cook's family.

From 27th Jan, my own art department at Queen Mary's School, Mon-Sat 11-12.40

Jan. 1964

[to Papa] I was ill in bed for a few days & the cook carried on without bothering me, & did special dishes to tempt me

to eat … I can just imagine you in your studio, with snow on the roofs opposi te… Pleased the Nehru pictures pleased —it really was terribly exciting.

As I write, the sun is shining but it is freezing inside the house. D has some students in the study, & so I am in the sitting room … It would make a world of difference if we had a fireplace, but we haven't, so we can only imagine log fires and roasting chestnuts.

D is so busy, & the other wives are practically all old enough to be my mother. I miss college friends more than I can tell, esp Janet & Sylvia.

Our garden is a desert as yet—nothing will be planted until later in the year. We have a hedge, but the cows keep eating it. It is actually supposed to be a variety they don't like, but they seem to have other ideas.

Jan. 1964

[to Mama] Am pleased you refer to 'when' you come.

Can just imagine busy little Yarm, a bit cold and blustery, perhaps an edging of snow between the sets & bright sunshine with clouds covering it every few seconds.

We eat practically all European food. This is perfectly normal … *[food prices listed]* We had a chicken which cooked down to a pigeon for about 8/-

So far, I haven't got the Dec. 'Housewife'. I'm just longing for it—I really do devour it when it comes.

We're going to a Hindu wedding this afternoon & a luncheon party on Sunday … both shd be v jolly.

I would love to go to Bombay and see the sea—I do miss it terribly. Apart from that redeeming factor, I think Bombay is horrible.

… Long to have a look round Binns … I shall go mad in C&A's basement when we do come home. You can come and help pick up the debris.

Jan. 30, 1964

[to Mama] We have both had odd bits of illness, from which we have rapidly recovered through the care of doctors at St. Stephen's Hospital … I've just come out of hospital this afternoon. We've just lost our first baby … I wasn't quite two months pregnant, so hadn't even started knitting! Please, please don't worry. Everyone has been terribly kind & I'm taking all sorts of medicines … we are both disappointed naturally … I should start school on Saturday, but that can wait another week.

Jan. 31, 1964

Dear Mama & Papa. Here is a letter to cheer away any gloom. Danny is looking after me so well. I can't tell you how wonderful he is … brought me communion in hospital.

Coll people are all so kind w visits & magazines & notes and advice to D … Today I sat out on the verandah for a couple of hours & a student came to cheer me up and help us to eat some Indian sweets (v sickly but delicious).

B Lal makes me eat, & today made me a stew w everything cooked in milk—'Good food for Madam' he says.

The friend I went to the University gardens with (she is half Russian) Melitza Srivastava, brought me flowers & gossip. Having had a similar experience, she is v sympathetic & full of good sense … have just read George Eliot, 'Scenes of Clerical Life' and am now engrossed in 'The Warden' by Trollope—can hear Papa saying 'You get more like your mother every day'!

Feb. 6, 1964

A lovely morning with birds singing & just a gentle warmth … to my right, a vase of marigolds, and another of pansies. Last week, we had roses & sweet peas. Dahlias are glorious here, and lots of glorious flowering shrubs.

I am now back in circulation, though D insists I put my feet up from time to time. He managed the house, argued w. cookie and did the shopping wonderfully.

Today we are going on our first spree to N Delhi for weeks. I start school on Monday … also teaching some elocution!

Today for lunch we are having meat pie followed by chocolate soufflé and cream—Longing to plan delicious smackerels for you! A jay has just perched on the garden fence. I have been having b'fast in bed this last week. Really, it is wonderful to have one's own servant, to be as ill as you like & not inconvenience anyone!

You did not tell me Nana had been ill this past winter. My dearest wish is to bring her a grandchild, so look after her, please ... another bird now, v bright green body, brilliant orange head & amber wings!

Will soon send dress instructions for ship &c, so you can start sewing or collecting or both!

On Saturday, going to a polo match with a crowd from coll. Sunday is a staff picnic, but neither of us wants to go —sounds really deadly.

By the way, I don't wear make-up—proper dowdy old missionary—toe nails brilliant pink.

Feb. 18, 1964

Am feeling v much better now, taking new dope containing alcohol—can feel the glow going down.

Now fully installed in school & all goes well—all the kids call the teachers 'Auntie'.

Polo match was splendid— British and Indian army teams—India won 6-4.

The other evening, we had the Sircars in for dinner, & last night a student ... the Bishop tonight.

Do you realise, we've been married for 6 months! Tried on wedding dress the other day, & it still fits!

Today, packing winter clothes away & taking out summer things ... The doc has advised and we shall prob. go to

Simla for part of the hot weather … I don't want to go, but I suppose it will be v jolly really.

Feb. 26, 1964

December 'Housewife' & calendar from Kath *[D's sister]* have just arrived—apparently such choice items usually disappear in the post.

We are thrilled the college gardeners have put loads & loads of flower pots on the verandahs, inc. Michaelmas daisies.

On Sat we went to the Delhi Flower Show—flowers fm all over the world, inc 'a host of golden daffs' fm England … Coll got quite a few prizes as ever.

Sunday—went on St. James Parish picnic, about 25 miles from Delhi, lots of delightful lakelets, w a gt variety of waterbirds. We are avid birdwatchers, & take binoculars everywhere … met a few folk I know at the High Commission, who were fishing & let us have a few casts … A group of nomads with laden donkeys passed, and a snake charmer with apprentice boy came and performed … camels turning water wheels … v colourful village women singing on their way to a wedding … On the way home, stopped at the Buddha Jayanti garden—carpets of flowers, surely the most beautiful garden in the world! … a thoroughly delightful day.

Last night, just as we were going to bed … dancers w drummers & pipes passed the house—to the servants quarters —beginning of the Holi celebration—since we are the only people living outside the inner gates, the noise was initially a bit scary!

School goes well, and art room gradually taking shape as I want it.

Chapel goes well Sunday Holy Communion, which D initiated, is well attended, & we usually have some boys in for breakfast afterwards—just like 18th century, b'fast parties!.

I've done quite a bit of baking—sausage rolls, jam tarts, custards, ginger biscuits, cheese straws, lemon-curd homemade sweets, v sickleberry but delicious.

Please ask the Vicar for the Order of Service for Easter Carol Service at St. Peter's 1963—by AIRMAIL immediately, please.

Had to visit the the courts for a document y'day & saw prisoners in terrible chains.

Diary for coming week - Sun we go out to tea … Mon Prayer meeting (ugh!) in chapel & tea at the house for 20-30 … I give dinner party in the evening (Shanklands) … Tues have a friend to tea … Thurs another friend to lunch & tea (Miss Gotch, whom we'd met on the Caledonia) … Sat to tea at the Brotherhood—EVERYONE was there, if you see what I mean … + some school of course!

Take care in the cold! God bless. Fondest love.

March 9, 1964

No Goya book yet, or Gazettes. Things do take an age.

Thank you for both letters. It really does delight us to hear from you both. It is v interesting to hear of your painting experiments, Papa.

We are both v well, though it is beginning to feel a bit HOT. We now have ceiling fans in the house.

Am enjoying school v much, & the classes seem to be, too. D takes me on the scooter & collects me each day, and lunch is ready when we come back, so all is running smoothly.

On Sun 1st, we went to tea w an ex-principal of my school, a rich old lady who is v sweet … she presented me with an embroidered hanky for being her 'first visitor to Bethany *[her cottage]* from St Stephen's'.

Y'day to a coll clerk's house for their sons' (Hindu) initiation … head shaved, bathed, new clothes, garlands—delicious Indian food.

I made some potted meat the other day, & we are drinking homemade lemon cordial. Am also knitting D a sweater in 4-ply—can you imagine!

D is out to coffee tonight w W Cantwell Smith—nice family.

14 March 1964

How much is beef in England ?—I do look forward to England—how are Pussy, the Merrywethers, Yarm Market? Tell Anne Merrywether to get herself to college (not too near home) and let her hair down—she'll never get a better chance!

Thank you for report of Janet's wedding. I am so pleased you went & seemed to enjoy yourself, Mummy.

I shall be alone most of this weekend as D is leading a Quiet Day at St. Stephen's Community

Y'day a man came round the houses and we bought a musical instrument … an itar, such a jolly 'folk' thing.

Could you please send some patterns for me … because we are again expecting a baby, at the end of the year.

My flower seeds are all up now—they grow at a terrific rate—dying for end of rains to plant out the veg garden. For the past two mornings, we have had lots of green parrots in the garden. Cookie says 'Much pollies come'. He continues to be a gem, but the sweeper is no good so am sacking him.

I am trying to sell some articles about India—prices are v high on food. There is v little sugar to be had, & no flour, not even Black Market. Rice is also v expensive. There are no rupees to spare, so planning is v tricky.

April 6, 1964

School is now on summer timetable, 7.50-11.30. For me, 8 hours teaching per week … salary of Rs.226 = £17-7-6 per month—v high by Indian standards.

D is out this evening at Bishop's meeting—I will take evensong in the chapel.

D says I look about 16—wonder if Mama's agelessness has set in with me—hope so.

It is so nice when all sorts just pop in.

Birthday present … you know the sort of things I like—nothing serious or intelligent, please! I spend 364 days being that! If it is wearable, let it not be too 'sensible'.

We now have our own lizards, and the Principal's dog has adopted us and often drops in for breakfast. He goes to chapel every day, even when the Principal does not.

We now have Indian food for lunch, complete with chapattis—all v delicious. On Sun. I made a lot of fruit drinks —lemon, apple, grapefruit, lime. We also have 'Cokes' in the fridge—not the same as coal in the bath.

I now know about 50 Hindi words—I asked the cook in Hindustani today to bring me one small hot chapatti with butter—how about that!

Had an Easter card and long letter from Miss Millburn *[Juliet's Stockton headmistress]*

April 16, 1964

You've no idea how much we lk fwd to your letters. Still no Goya book.

Temp now 75-105

We had a small dinner party last night—delicious Indian food except for pudding, fruit salad in sponge. whipped cream. Everyone had seconds!

Out to tea … our hostess showed me how to wear a sari … deliciously comfortable, & they hide all sorts of tyres and bulges. Am now looking forward to my own.

No money in UK bank—may we open an account with you?.

April 29, 1964

D & I went fishing in the Jumna with some friends—they gave us two huge fish wh we grilled in butter.

A coffee and goody party with 4 1st year African students from Nyasaland *[soon to be Malawi]*, a v jolly evening.

25th Ladies Night in college, smashing 'nosh-up'

26th D taking services at St Thomas, New Delhi.

Bought my first sari—diaphanous, gorgeously trimmed, 'shot' red & green … sewing a blouse i.e. bare midriff … tomorrow we are having a dinner party & I hope to wear it.

On the 4th, we are going to a farewell party for a young English member of staff, John Haysom.

6th - to Brotherhood, celebrating the Ascension

9th - an engagement party

13th - a young VSO girl, friend of Paul Lucas, is coming to stay overnight on way to Simla

Daddy's telescope sounds terrific … Hope you get to Edinburgh at festival time.

We live in a v English, 'normal' world but half a mile away there are poor coolies, exhausted & often deformed through hard work, and doing animals' work hauling great heavy loads on their backs. They never have enough to eat, sleep on the street and have hardly any clothing. In fact they only live to about 30. Life is desperate. Our cook has lost 5 children, and a child's funeral procession is common … Poverty makes it necessary to overload animals and work in terrible heat to make the most of each job. Children of 6 or 7 go to work. This is India.

May 20, 1964

[D's sister Kath's wedding in Darlington] We had Holy Communion in college chapel in the morning, went back there & read the marriage service and hymns at 11 a.m. GMT—4.30 p.m. IST and had a special wedding tea, & on Sunday a chicken lunch to celebrate—did all we could save be there in body.

Put Paul Lucas' friend on train to Simla—she travelled ordinary 3rd class—it was worse than a cattle truck, v v squashed, hard seats all night.

.

[offered art teaching at British & French schools]

Indian artist friend, Ernest Joseph, 50ish, shaven head, monocle, took us to artist-material shops in Chandni Chowk and stocked up for Simla—watercolour—wish I hadn't left my oils behind.

Tonight, we have a guest for dinner, & tomorrow one for lunch & dinner. The Bishop is dining with us on the 25th, so you see we never have a dull moment!
… longing for Binns, Marks &S, C&A.

May 24, 1964

Warmest Easter gr eetings. D is to take services at Hissar on Gd Friday, so I shall be alone. He leaves on Thurs morning and gets back Fri evening … we went to a service at the hospital, blessing of a new building.

The great news is that I have a <u>studio</u> in the 2nd bedroom, with tables & shelves made from scooter crate—also shelves for pantry & a dressing table from the wood. At this precise moment, the sweeper is kneading clay for me.

Last week v busy:-
Sunday - out to luncheon party. Dr.. Bouquet & 1 student to tea
Monday - Chamber music concert (Tubingen) with another couple, & home to us for dinner … vgood, Vivaldi … Bach … Grieg … Mozart

Tues - lunch at the Brotherhood
- a friend of mine home to tea
Wednesday - to the airport to see off Dr.. Bouquet
Thus - D out to univ dinner
Sat - a farewell party at the Workmans (going back to Calcutta)—all v smart w lovely booze and gorgeous food. We left at 11.45 p.m. and had to make our way back to Old Delhi (15 miles). All went well until we came to a road diversion … round by the big mosque & the thieves market— we were terrified. We also had to avoid the Ridge because of dacoits. How nice to arrive home safely.

May 27, 1964

Dreadful news of the death of Nehru on BBC … a dreadful blow to everyone here.

Wed 20 - Fr. Sharp, Head of Brotherhood, to dinner
Fri - an African student friend, Fred Magezi from Uganda, to lunch & dinner.
25th - 2 young lecturers dropped in for coffee *[this became the 'bachelors' evenings', with younger members of staff inviting themselves or being invited for a convivial evening usually in the garden]*.
26th - An Anglo-Indian friend for coffee, & the Bishop for dinner
27th - an Indian friend for lunch & to the B'hood for dinner
31st - a friend of D's from Darlington! for supper—and on the 1st we go to Simla. D got up at 4 a.m. on 21st to go to station by 4.30 to queue for tickets for Simla … the only way to go anywhere!

We have bought good fishing rods for equiv of 18/6 each—and 2 dress lengths to keep me quiet!

We now buy our tea from a tea dealer in the nearby bazaar, Kamla Nagar, and get a lovely brew for only 6/- a lb.

Babu Lal brings me a lovely dish of fresh jasmine flowers every morning—they smell heavenly.

The sweets here have <u>real silver</u> on them

A great disappointment—the film of all the photos since we came here has been destroyed in the processing.

We have a big pumpkin growing in the garden (coach & 4?) ... a couple of dust storms and a thunderstorm.

Simply devouring books ... Victoria, lots of history, Northanger Abbey.

I do love entertaining, esp at short notice ... people just come & invite themselves to lunch—we can usually cope.

YMCA, Simla Punjab—June 3, 1964

... about 8,000 feet above sea level (Delhi 400) ... lovely pine forests & snow-covered peaks in the distance ... here until the 14th, then move to Prospect Lodge.

Simla is a fantastic place—the great mountainous countryside dominates the town, which perches precariously.

We had a 3rd cl. Sleeper fm Delhi, v comfortable, to Kalka, then a taxi up to Simla ... tremendous climb, hairpin bends, w gt chasms below ... stopped at Solan for tea &

toast (lovely country butter). Wild roses at the roadside, just like home until you glanced at the view beyond! The YM is barely furnished, with communal tables, but holidaying Stephanians can fill a whole table, and the food is good, Indian of course. Service is good, room bearer brings morning tea ... We've just come from a walk to Prospect Lodge, wh is gorgeous.

Delhi has been v hot—115 ... D went in the 2-million crowd to see the procession to Nehru's cremation ... on Sunday we went to the cremation platform with jasmine from the college garden. We are pleased Shastri is the new P.M. (He was at the reception when we met Nehru).

Babu Lal is living in our house with some of his family, so all will be safe & they will have a gd holiday away fm their cramped quarters at the Jesuit school ... Our sweeper, who is about 15, has just been married to a 7-yr old girl! They will not live together for years. ... 2,000 rupees and much dried fruit in the dowry.

My hair is lovely & long now—D calls me Gloria.

Please send parish news.

Simla has wonderful peaches, apricots.

June 9, 1964 YMCA Simla

There is so much to tell you ... It will be a 'snippets' letter.

One evening, we passed a little fruit shop, where the proprietor was singing religious scriptures by the light of a lamp ... beautiful Tibetan-type faces ... Some of them are coolies and they carry fantastic loads up these ghastly hills ... In most of Simla, no cars are allowed, so there are genuine rickshaws (running men, 4 to a rickshaw) ... lots of silver monkeys with black faces—I didn't think monkeys could be pretty but these were lovely ... D has bought a lovely cherrywood walking stick, & he looks v nice on country walks—there is a special wood bazaar here ... I shall pbby do you a sky map, Papa—the sky is so big here—we have seen The Plough, but not Orion yet ... We found a wonderful junk shop, lots of animal heads on shields, old Brit.Raj. photos ... On a picnic with a lecturer friend the other day, we found wild strawberries & they were lovely. Flowers found: violets, star of Bethlehem, daisies, celandines, Christmas roses, veitch, coltsfoot & a few others ... all the flowers were finished weeks ago in Delhi, climbing roses, hollyhocks, pansies ... a lovely walk among hills & pine trees, and saw in the distance snow-covered mountains which I think were Tibet ... I am looking for a v small fir tree to take back to Delhi to plant for Christmas.

Can you imagine, I have actually a sunburnt face, and even in this short time feel a different person since we left Delhi ... Wonderful not to be dripping with sweat all the time. I am actually wearing at this moment my blue wool dress!

The architecture here is funny—Mock-Tudor, even the Town Hall ... a Victorian bandstand on the Mall, where 'the youngsters' (you see, I'm a married woman !!) parade in the evening—only when you get into the bazaar you see lovely carved Indian archways.

Please remember us both to all the kind folk who ask after us. How I miss Shredded Wheat, Wheatabix, Kitkat,

Fry's cream bars—Indian sweets are delicious but I do miss bars of things—a tube of Smarties costs 3/- here—D sometimes buys them as a special treat, I keep them in the fridge and eat one a day

Prospect Lodge, June 16, 1964

Have just finished 'Adam Bede' & now reading another Trollope & a book on Van Gogh & more Thackeray. ... still a Galsworthy, another Trollope, & books on Wm Morris and Le Corbusier on my holiday shelf.

Just bought and will send you a Nehru commemorative stamp, Papa.

Returning to British School as art teacher next term, so I shall have 2 jobs—the extra £sd will be useful.

Tell Ann Merrywether I have bought her an Indian doll from Himachal Pradesh—the costume is v gay.

Hope Nana will be alright—make her wear my big dressing gown over her clothes when she sits by the fire at night.

D much enjoys the letters fm both of you. Please more news of St. Peter's, send Gazettes, parish magazine.

June 27, 1964

Thursday—Shopping to buy a few Kashmiri trinkets ... a v pretty white necklace painted with flower designs ... a small lacquered box for my dressing table ... small embroidered drawstring bag, just the thing for keys, hanky and collection on Sunday—expedition finished with lemonade/ice cream.

Friday—out to dinner w an Indian friend from Delhi at Davicos, which is the 'hot spot' in town with band and dancing—including the Twist!

Saturday—the VSO who stayed with us in Delhi is now working at a Tibetan refuge, so we went to see her—the medical in charge is fm St. Stephen's Hospital in Delhi & had nursed me—we took a picnic & walked about 7 miles through pine forests. There are 150 tiny Tibetan children and some adults. Fortunately, we were brought back to Prospect Lodge in the jeep, so didn't have to walk another 7 miles!

I weigh 7st 4lbs—ridiculous I am 5'5" and weighed 9st 6lbs last October. I am now taking malt and rattling w vitamin pills.

It is lovely to relax in the coolness here, but I <u>dread</u> going back to Delhi, being nearly dead when we got here! This morning v early, we had a huge thunderstorm, and it poured down. Most of the buildings here, including Prospect Lodge, have tin roofs & the rain sounds terrific on them.

Simla, July 7, 1964

The other day, we walked to a milestone which said in Hindi 'Tibet 197' !!!

Y'day we had a gt thrill—early in the morning we had a phone call to say it was the Dalai Llama's birthday, and in 20 minutes a Land Rover would call to take us to the Tibetan nursery ... all the children were in their best clothes & seated beside an altar, on which was a scarf-draped picture of the DL and a 4-tier cake made of rice and sugar. The 2 lamas were in their best clothes—the young one brought us traditional buttered tea—rather nice ... also some of the rice and sugar concoction, also v nice. After the children had eaten their fill, there was singing and dancing, and each child placed a white scarf, given by the lama, on the altar, and touched it w their forehead. The grownups knelt and touched the ground with their fore-heads before the altar. Everyone danced, and there was a fire to keep away evil spirits ... a v pleasant day, and before we left, we actually shook hands w the junior lama.

The monsoon has broken in Simla ... tremendous storms and Prospect Lodge is up in the clouds.

Have just finished 'Mill on the Floss' and started Gals-worthy's 'Fraternity'—my 7th bk in 5 weeks ... have finished D's sweater and my 2nd dress & have started on a table cloth of drawn-thread work.

Have gained 2 lbs in 10 days, so now 7st 6lbs fully clothed ... have cut my hair in prep for Delhi—D claims I look about 18.

Delhi, July 11, 1964

When we got home fm Simla, it was pouring down. The house was spotless, & all the shopping done, & we've got a garden exactly as we planned it & it is lovely *[sketch map provided]*.

Just before we left Simla, we had coffee with Mrs. Betjeman, wife of John the poet! She is the image of her husband …. had been on a pony trek in the mountains.

We've just had a delicious roast buffalo lunch & a chilled egg custard. Think I'll make a few cheese straws for tea.

We've got a new dhobi due instead of the college 'Jack the Ripper'. Until then, D is doing the heavy laundry.

I slept like a log on the train coming here, but D was awake prac all night fighting to keep the bugs off me—in swarms, vile creatures.

The weather now is v sticky and I have a v sticky face all day. I envy you your Edinburgh holiday—say hello there for me.

Work starts on Wed (I leave home at 7), so I shall get the house 'rolling' in the next few days.

Delhi, July 21, 1964

Both in full swing with our jobs—enjoying my 2 jobs, but Q Mary school admin is a mess.

The weather is ghastly—82-96, but not so much the heat as the dampness, just soaking and dripping all the time. When you come, Mama, it shd be cooling down. Do hope you are saving like fury. I shall send wardrobe instructions soon. The thinnest non-sheer cotton is the answer.

Gosh I do hope Uncle Bill can come.

Our neighbours (in the other new house) the Aryas, are v nice. She is borrowing my iron, and I her sewing machine.

We have just bought the following from the seeds wallah: cauliflower, cabbage, brussels sprouts, French & broad beans, lettuce, carrots, turnips, parsley, tomatoes—and cornflowers, sweet peas, hollyhocks, nasturtiums. Isn't it exciting.

I've done a bit of baking, but its hot work with no fan in the kitchen … apple pies, delicious brown bread.

Some lovely birds in the garden—green bee-eaters, v elegant, and two golden orioles in the neem tree, brilliant yellow & a piercing cry.

… looking fwd to news of Janet's & Carol's weddings.

Delhi, August 1, 1964

We have had 3 letters from you recently.

5 p.m.—the gardener is mowing the lawn and there is a lovely grassy smell … having tea (brown bread & apricot jam, apple) … we were invited out to tea, but I have a heavy cold, so D has gone on his own, wh he hates—he is v kind—5 mins after he left, he came back to ask me to lock the front door to make him feel happier.

We've just bought a doormat, hope to have a carpet before you come *[we never did, only dhurries]*

Food prices are terribly high—rice, dall, potatoes, veg almost doubled since before the holiday, and we are having an economy campaign.

Have just discovered Cookie can make fabulous crisps, so we are just about living on them to his gt amusement.

... a swarm of dragonflies continuously hovering over the garden. We have turned the Visitors Book into a bird book also—over 15 different birds come to the garden.

This is the season for white ants, and our woodwork is riddled with them—the contractor is coming to replace some woodwork.

Looking fwd to starting on Monday more work at QM from 9 to 15 hours p.w.
 – still-life, figure drawing and composition in the senior school.

Temp in 90s, but damp, our clothes smell musty & horrible. I now weigh 8st 2lbs.

Delhi, August 8, 1964

Thank you for the lovely birthday card—wish you could send Smarties [equivalent of 4/6 a tube here now!]

We are kept jolly busy. At QM have been asked to do costumes for Speech Day play, and Coll have asked me to design scenery for a play, and help with costumes for another, 'Mad About Men'... The new Fine Arts Society in coll want me to teach modelling and pottery ... am supervising new clay room, and selecting art magazines for the coll reading room. Just wish there were more hours in the day because it is imposs to rush about in the heat.

Six nationalities in Chapel on Sunday—Indian, English, Ugandan, Japanese, West Indian, Russian.

Nice your new microscope, Papa—you wd perhaps appreciate some of our horrible insects!

We've just had the roof tarred and felted as the inside walls were in an awful soggy mess with the monsoon.

Veg seeds which I sowed 2/3 days ago are now up!
20,000 jobs to do this morn, including making sausage rolls, ice cream and tomato juice.

Delhi, Aug. 22, 1964

Now teaching only in senior school at QM, & enjoying it v much—Br Sch as usual—doing costumes for another school play.

I'm mad about fruit—sometimes 4 apples a day 2 oranges or sweet limes; & there are lovely juicy pears, plums and grapes at present.

We've had a hectic week:-
Mon 17th, our wedding anniversary, went to HC w D at Community, and after school a taxi trip to ND, a bit of shopping and a gorgeous tea—I had a double sundae and gosh did I feel sick!
Tues—our artist friend Ernest Joseph to dinner and he brought me a gorgeous Windsor & Newton watercolour

box—made in Eng and v swish. He just saw it in Mysore & thought it wd make a lovely prize!

Wed—Brit Sch staff meeting, & lunch w a ND friend—gorgeous house, beer w lunch! And tea w another ND friend—cake—luxury because we can't get flour.

Mrs. Sircar sent me a lovely basket crib for as long as we need it—the baby is due about a week after Christmas—we didn't tell you earlier because I was so poorly in Simla and we wondered whether all wd again be lost. I am now v healthy

Thurs—inaugural tea of the SCM (Student Christian Movement) followed by chapel service.

I ordered material fm an art dealer for the new Fine Art Society in college

Fri—had a rest!

Sat—consultation about the college Shaw play, 'You Never Can Tell'—helping w scenery, props, etc

Sat—Cookie came home with a great prize—a kilo of flour! So I made a belated Bero anniversary fruit cake (I've been saving currants—1/6 per ounce), and a meat and potato pie and a few jam tarts.

Just off to make a cheese flan.

Delhi, Aug. 29, 1964

I have just realised that today you are off on your jolly hols to Edinburgh ... we long and long for Scotland and the Northumberland coast ... spit on the Heart [of Midlothian] for me, Mama!.

No school this Saturday, so programme is: 7.20 D rises for chapel at 7.40, 7.30 I have b'fast in bed and give Cookie shopping list and meal orders. 8-11 housework, washing etc. 11 coffee and letter-writing. Lunch 1 p.m. , then feet up, after 3 to local bazaar, veg & fruit stalls are like walking round an agricultural show, so beautifully set out. In the evening, a bit of gardening—D says take it easy and says I am a compulsive worker.

The garden and the lawn are gorgeous, and not a weed in sight. In the sitting room, I've put orange flowers in that brown coffee jug that Nana gave me.

Delhi, Sept. 8, 1964

… how thrilled we are about Uncle Bill coming *[on a business trip to E & W Pakistan]* please tell him HE CAN STAY AS LONG AS HE LIKES, as it is no extra work for me as we have servants *[long list of items to bring, including Marathon nappies, plastic baby pants, etc]* …. please ask D's Mama for D's christening robe—we would love to use it … thermos flask filled w Smarties and Dolly Mixtures We need the baby things above all else.

Delhi, Sept. 11, 1964

We were thrilled with all your letters from Edinburgh— we were positively green w envy.

1 Sept—to the Bird Watching Society, v interesting & entertaining
3 Sept—paid all last month's bills!
4 Sept—open lecture on the Biological Clock
5 Sept—shopping for cotswool for tiny winter night-dresses! … have now made 2, one with embroidered daisies and little white star flowers, tied with pink ribbons, another

has cornflowers and blue ribbons (buttercups come next). Have also knitted bootees and cardigan.

8 Sept—went to Commonwealth Women's Assocn handicrafts sale at Br High Commission w Elspeth Shankland—all the types you would expect! Bought a few things for January. D collected me and the little scooter was v proud to go down the Rajpath and by India Gate. In the evening, D and I went to 2 thrilling Hiking Club films.

9 Sept—a snake in the garden the other night! An English friend called for tea and brought me some lovely packets of Eng flower seeds she had smuggled in. It is just about the time to plant.

[lengthy advice for mothers' visit—'clothes for India']

Delhi, Sept. 19, 1964

Both your last letters and one from D's Mama arrived at the same time, so we had a lovely little orgy.

On Thursday a clergy friend to tea & dinner after talking to SCM, and y'day we went to the college play—I was asked at the last minute to make a false nose—Indians never think of things until the 11th hour—also busy on flower headdresses for school play.

On Saturday, the Sircars took us shopping in New Delhi by car, and treated us to tea—wasn't that kind!

D is working terribly hard—to 1 or 2 every night. Thank goodness we have good hols.

I've just had a rise of £1 per month = £18-7-6 … extremely well paid by Indian standards … Living is so terribly expensive, and we don't know how we shall manage when I stop work. We are far worse off than SPG missionaries ... We can't afford the dentist ... my 48 hours in hospital cost £8, a big hole. If one of us had an op., on the face of it we would have to die, though we assume coll wd help. Everyone of course expects me to continue to work and have an ayah, but we don't think that right—we are regarded as slightly cracked!

Cookie got some black market flour last week, so we had chocolate cake and apple pie.

D is becoming a little unbearable as the UK election approaches. We don't exactly agree & neither will budge an inch!!

PS There is a chameleon living in the tree at our front door.

Delhi, Sept. 26, 1964

24 hours continuous downpour, absolutely flat-out cats & dogs all the time ... its now deliciously cool and last night we needed a blanket.

Sorry, Papa, coming home for keeps is not as easy as you think—3 1/2 years just isn't long enough for this sort of work, and it really doesn't depend much on our feelings for England.

... now 6 tomato plants in pots—they smell delicious.

The full moon looked wonderful the other night—v brilliant & clear and surrounded by dusty grey clouds like the beach when the tide goes out. We often think of you on our way from chapel because here all the stars are out by 7.30 p.m. Wish you cd see the gorgeous clear starry nights … the weather is now most pleasant, w heavy dew in the morn that sparkles like frost

On Thursday we had a Roman Catholic priest to dinner, one of the local Jesuits—a most pleasant evening … ham risotto from the Good Housekeeping cook book.

We often plan future hols in Scotland and on the continent with the proceeds of my teaching, with soapbox-furniture in the vicarage.

Managed to borrow latest Sunday Times & Observer fm the Brit School—delicious. I have finished Trollope 'Last Chronicle' (900 pages) and feel quite lost as I have read all in that series.

2 Oct—I have retired!!! … we go to Agra tomorrow until Monday.

Delhi, Oct. 14, 1964

Canadian couple and little boy staying—the boy, 4 years is a horror, w v bad manners, rowdy, rude, and the mother inconsiderate. As D & I say, they are not British and so presumably do not know the niceties.

Agra, 4 1/2 hours by train—D was allowed 1st cl + Rs 5 for extras, and this covered both our return fares 2nd cl. (rather than the ghastly fight in 3rd cl.) & taxi to station.
Stayed at St. John's College.

On Sunday, D went over to the Cantonment Church—as it meant travelling by rickshaw, I had the morning off—then he gave address for Christian staff. The college is 'Victorian Mughal' w a huge assembly hall—D spoke at end of term service—the hall was packed & his address good.

Monday—up early by the college car to the TAJ MA-HAL wh looked lovely in the bright sunlight. The inlay work is incredible but the interior is rather melancholy. When it was complete, the hands of all those who made the beautiful inlay work were chopped off !! ... on to Agra fort ... huge, beautiful marble rooms and inlay tiles in the most gorgeous semi-precious stones ... the Shah's bathroom is fab—just the place for lounging around in diaphanous pyjamas ... To a smaller tomb, Itmad ud daulah, much prettier, more delicate ... v ancient paintings of flowers, sort of gesso I think. From there, to the river, where we fed turtles with huge flashing eyes—they were lovely ... beside a Hindu temple w a huge red god and a huge black god draped in red ... horrible faces. The red god had an electric fan turning above him—to placate him? We bought a peacock feather fan for 4 1/2d. ... saw a lovely elephant with painted face and ears.

Caught 4.30 p.m. train home after a lovely weekend.

Delhi, Oct. 18, 1964

Well, Labour has done it ... most exciting!

Janet & I keep in touch regularly ... just had a letter fm Sylvia, who hopes to visit you at Christmas.

Food parcels—a v kind thought, but either it wd never reach us, or we wd have crippling duty to pay. Food still v expensive—we have one vegetarian meal every day.

2 new English lecturers have arrived, Allan Privett & Wm Crawley, and brought me Smarties from the ship's shop.

Y'day shopping … we bought a baby bath & nappies.

The gardeners brought me a huge bunch of golden rod … have it everywhere in the house.

Weather is lovely now, and cool enough to wear makeup.

Thank you for Parish Chronicle and Gazettes—a miracle that they made it. 'Housewife' hardly ever makes it.

Mama, have you booked your passage yet?

Delhi 21 Oct 1964

… Information for Uncle Bill … Gosh, how excited we are! If UB sends a telegram, it must be Express—thousands of ordinary just get put in the post.

Now 'retired' from both schools *[pregnancy advancing]*.

Delhi, Oct. 27, 1964

Uncle Bill … marvellous if he cd bring 2 pkts of almond icing

We've just filled out a form to say we need 10lbs of sugar per month (Us +Cookie & sweeper) but are told we will only get 4lbs. *[next day]* got 2 extra kilos from college.

This morn I spent hours taking out warm clothes & packing away cottons.

Have got Dr. Spock book but hardly ever have time for exercises and to relax ... today I go for a check up. Last night, I had an X-ray, and now we have an exciting picture of a perfect baby! I can see little fingers and toes and a beautiful head and back. The table I had made is being converted into a 'baby unit'.

D & I are going to a film in college, and after dinner (which I am partly cooking) he has a confirmation class. We are kept pretty busy!

In the sitting room, I have put a v light, dainty variety of Michaelmas daisies in that black teapot you brought me from Stockton market!

D asks whether you cd send one or two copies of the new newspaper, The Sun.

Delhi 9 Nov.9, 1964

He's been !—just like Santa on Christmas morning— Uncle Bill !! The door bell rang, & I heard someone ask for Padre Sahib O'Connor—he'd sent a cable, but it hadn't arrived, so he did—completely out of the blue. He had a couple of days w nothing to do in Karachi, and thought he'd just pop over! A wonderful surprise, and my, what a haul *[list of many presents, baby equipment, etc]* We really are overwhelmed, and when we woke on Sunday morn, cd not believe Uncle Bill was just in the next room. We took him round the University & generally pottered, but he's coming back for 2 or 3 days later on, so we can 'do' Delhi. He mended a light wh had been faulty for months, and bought us an electric fire! He is so kindly & says all the right 'uncley' things

Friday—went to QM school to help with play.

Delhi, Nov 1964

Last Sat, went to St. Thomas' Garden Fete, where D said an opening prayer before Lady Gore-Booth (wife of High Comm) cut the ribbon. He as you know hates fetes, but I just love them, & it was pleasant to see lots of people we don't see often (St. Thomas' is in N Delhi). The next day, Sunday, was St. James fete—our parish church—we gave ourselves a treat and bought a sponge cake made by someone at the High Comm.—we haven't seen flour since June, but they are obviously not so afflicted!

Tues. the curator of the new oriental museum at Durham gave a lecture in college, and D brought him home for coffee.

Wed. went for my check-up, and horror of horrors, I now weigh 10st. Dr. has ordered strict rest and potions and injections. I do get rather weary, but I don't much like sitting about even then!

Thank you for yr letter, Papa—you do seem to be v busy —wish I cd see all your paintings.

Mon Tues Wed I am invigilating some exams, so shd get a bit of pocket money. I do hope we can wangle a bit of black mkt flour & save enough sugar to make a Christmas cake.

I have finished a little patchwork quilt, & Cookie is getting me cotton for the stuffing.

Do take care in the cold. Its freezing here, too.

Delhi, Nov. 30, 1964

I've moved round the sitting-room furniture so that we can accommodate the electric fire, & yday, with dusk and frosty-type coldness outside, and the table-lamp and fire inside, we had for tea, brown bread & apple jam and read the Gazette and Echo—playing at being in England. It is now cold enough for 3 blankets & the white bedspread.

Last Thurs we were invited to tea w the PM's cousin, Mr Brijlal Nehru—I didn't feel like going, but D went—at tea, he declined an invitation to an evening w the President of India and went to a meeting in college w Krishna Menon !! *[ex-Minister of Defence]*

Tonight is 'Dinner night' in college, with the Primate (Anglican Archbishop) of Canada as chief guest. I am going to dinner with his wife … there are many other functions, but I am fighting for retirement.

I'm making what was to be baby unit curtain, but will hang it on the wall—appliqué embroidery, all the animals going to visit Vishnu *[sketch]*

Take care in the frost & snow & rain.

Delhi, Dec. 6, 1964

Thank you for the offer of a Christmas cake, but we would have to pay terrific duty, as we did last year. I am trying to save some sugar and will make a cake with atta (chapatti flour). We bought a piece of imitation holly to put on it, and an imitation Christmas tree and some candles and baubles, so we shd have a jolly though quiet time.

Because of rising prices, we have had to stop our monthly book allowance, but I am getting a book for Christmas about Japanese paper folding—origami.

The roses are coming out, and we have marigolds & lupins & cornflowers planted & I'm longing to see them bloom ... tomatoes have flowered. We had a mongoose in the garden the other day—I would love one as a pet, they look so sweet.

The lady next door is expecting a baby this month, so the din in January should be wonderful.

Tuesday. Well, Uncle Bill came just after we'd eaten his Sunday lunch! He'd been back to Lahore and all over the place ... had several punctures out in the wilds and went through one village where the men came out with guns. He's had terrific adventures but is always so calm ... is going to Kanpur & Calcutta & will be back on Friday—until Tuesday. D had to go to Founder's Day on Monday morn, so U Bill did some gardening, transplanting cabbages.

Delhi, Dec. 9, 1964

Last night a tremendous thunderstorm ... the garden this morn looks lovely & green & bright, but it is cold & breezy…two bulbuls are perched on the chrysanths, pecking off the petals.

I have packed things into my hospital case! We've just bought a dear little lamp with a dark red silk shade to provide soft light for getting up in the night to see to the infant

What lovely calendars you have sent, Papa, one with a picture of Sleights! *[Yorkshire village]* We are going to hang one in the study and one in the bedroom so we will wake to an English scene.

I now have a mirror on the dressing table, bought with birthday money given by the African student who is our personal friend, Fred Magezi. It was v sweet of him.

Tues 15th - Uncle Bill has just left. On Friday, we did some gardening and then huddled over the fire—it has been freezingly cold ... On Sat, a bit of shopping & sightseeing w U Bill, and he treated us to a super lunch at one of the best hotels in India. We actually had alcohol—D had beer, UB gin & tonic, and I had <u>Bristol Cream</u> sherry—a gorgeous meal—waiters wearing white gloves, etc—a lovely day altogether.

Sun - to our delight, UB came to chapel with us, & then, between huddles over the fire, he did more gardening, planting out the lettuce. We had sandwiches w some of the lettuce.

Mon - more shopping & another lovely luncheon treat, home for a last evening- & UB put a safe new flex on the electric fire. We had a celebration dinner of chicken pillau—I did a table decoration with fabulous gold flowers to go with the dinner service and a candle, so it was a pre-Christmas Christmas feast with a person from home.

In the evening, U Bill packed our gifts for you and others. It has been a lovely visit.

D is going to put a fresh coat of paint on the baby's crib.

Delhi, Dec. 20, 1964

Well, now you must surely have had yr report from Uncle Bill. We had a letter written in the air and we were v thrilled to hear fm him en route. Since he left, we have been to a JCR entertainment and had the Chapel carol service—we decorated the chapel & put up the crib & our tiny Christmas tree. The chapel was full (60-70) with extra seating. I'm sure everyone enjoyed it. I have been busy making paper angels wings for the Sunday School nativity play next Tuesday.

On Fr I had my check-up and the Dr. was v pleased … b.pressure back to normal … so you can tell Uncle Bill he must have done a power of good.

We have got some flour for our Christmas cake. Cookie was on the trail for about 4 days before he got some—he was coming away from the shop when a policeman stopped him and looked in his bag. Seeing the flour, the policeman asked 'Have you any money?' Cookie had Rs.2, change fm shopping. The policeman took it & sent cookie on his way. With the Bero recipe, we've got 2 cakes, one for Christmas and one for the christening. D did practically all the stirring.

Raisins are unknown here, so we put in cherries, assorted peels, walnuts, almonds, sultanas, nutmeg & currants.

Y'day, an English teacher whom we had met in Simla and works in New Delhi, Evelyn Reading, arrived out of the blue and asked to stay for lunch & tea. We were v pleased she felt able to ask—she gets rather depressed with her accommodation & food. She has made a most beautiful crochet-work shawl for the baby. An old Anglo-Indian teacher we had met at Sircars, also called, so we had quite a party for tea.

We are making up a hamper for Cookie—chicken, rice, fruit, nuts etc., etc. We plan to have in for tea on Christmas Day any students we find who haven't been able to get home—I shall make sausage rolls and fruit flans.

From both of us, fondest love & very best wishes for a happy, hearty and holy Christmas. We shall be thinking of you constantly. Please say a special prayer for Indian Christians—there will soon be one in the family!

Delhi, Boxing Day 1964

On Christmas Eve, D & I went shopping, and treated ourselves to a Kashmere rug wh looks v smart and cosy in the sitting room. ...our grocer had holly and mistletoe and we put some in the sitting room ... among decorations, I made a mobile with paper angels. In the evening we went with the two new Eng lecturers to a meal at Shanklands and to listen to the Kings College carols.

D helped at the midnight communion at St James and brought me communion home—we had a lovely little altar beside the crib, and afterwards cut the cake, about 2 a.m.

We had stockings with all the right stocking things! D had to go back to 8 a.m. at St. James and 11 at St Thomas. Cookie had the day off, but most things were already prepared & I cooked lunch. ... 8 students came to tea—we had cocktail-type things and my baking. After Chapel evensong, we just flopped & had a quiet read—we were too tired for supper, so we made tea and listened to the radio in bed.

D had H.C. this morning for St. Stephen's Day ... we expect a couple of visitors later, but really our entertaining has now stopped until after the baby... a wonderful & most happy Christmas in our new home (if you remember, we were still at Sircars last Christmas!)

* * * * *

WE ARE PARENTS

Delhi, Jan. 5, 1965

We are awaiting this procrastinator with mounting excitement. Saw my doctor this morning & we are now taking steps to encourage your grandchild to have a birthday … sorry for funny handwriting, but I am sunbathing in the garden—not too hot, but enough to get a gentle tan.

Have just finished knitting a pair of bright orange pull-ups for the infant for Simla, and have started an overcoat—never thought I wd ever have such knitting stamina!
We've got tomatoes—only the size of a sixpence as yet. … but w eating our own lettuce … roses are lovely & we have 4 lilies out.

I strongly recommend Christopher Hibbert's 'The Court at Windsor'—if you have any royalist tendencies left after reading it, I disown you! Now starting C Bronte's 'Shirley'.

I do envy you the snow.

Telegram: Grandson for you, both very well. Danny

Delhi (St. Stephen's Hospital) Jan. 11, 1965

Well, isn't it amazing! D brought your telegram this morning. His name is Aidan Daniel … 8lbs 4oz (Indian babies range from 5-6lbs as a rule) … D is thrilled to bits … wonderful that he was born on D's birthday, 7 mins to midnight on 9th January. I had a very easy time, no pain, just hard work, and Dr. Roseveare said I was a model patient ... I didn't make one squeak! ... a forceps birth ... he gave a good yell .... D was able to be with me for about 3 hours.

The new labour-ward sister, a Yorkshirewoman, Mary Earnshaw, has adopted me. All the women here have their mothers-in-law with them, and she felt sorry for me ... at the moment he is sleeping peacefully in a crib at my side after having a little feed

Although 6 days late, this little chap was certainly worth waiting for.

Everyone in college is thrilled—so is Cookie.

Give his great grandparents my love.

D has just arrived, and is gazing at the infant as usual— he says that he looks like Winston Churchill. I really must stop writing, and see if D will talk to me as well as the baby.

Delhi, Jan. 23, 1965

Thank you so v v much for the most gorgeous flowers, red gladioli and two I have never seen before, white & yellow.

The Principal loaned us his car & driver & we left hospital in time for tea at home on Monday 18th .... At the moment, I am having my afternoon rest, & Aidan is in bed at my side fast asleep ... we have had several student friends along to see him, and Elspeth Shankland, but no staff members yet.

We are thinking of having baby food sent out, as even baby food made under licence here is adulterated … had home-grown turnips and they were delicious—cauliflowers will soon be ready.

Delhi, Jan. 31, 1965

Well, yr grandson yelled his way through most of last night, first with hunger & then with a bad tummy because he gobbled so dreadfully … He gives us the most wonderful smiles, but they are more at the air than us—the whites of his eyes are v blue, like mine.

[query about various food costs in UK - clearly Delhi prices v difficult]

Delhi, Feb. 8, 1965

Y'day was the Baptism, in the college chapel … about 40 guests … a v happy little gathering, and A behaved v well … he wore D's christening robe & looked v sweet … the Principal is a godfather, and, we hope *[by proxy]* Paul Lucas, and our new friend Evelyn Reading the godmother, v good churchwoman & v nice but a scream too! She gave him a £5 cheque & a silver spoon, and me a mustard spoon, the bowl made from a 2 anna George V piece. He also got several toys from admirers.

Feb. 16, 1965 We have borrowed a pram—carrycot on wheels.

A at 4 weeks weighed 10.6—he is growing at a fantastic rate—he'll be on to egg & chips in no time, at the rate he's going.

Delhi 21 Feb 1965

What smashing photographs … Mother, that is <u>exactly</u> the dress I dream of wearing. Are you bringing it to India? —what's more important, are you taking it back to England !!!

Yr grandson is bouncing. He chuckles and gurgles & blows bubbles … I made 3 tops & pants, now smocking them, wh I adore doing.

Aidan went to chapel this morning, and did a bit of singing & gurgling. D is preaching at St. Thomas church.

Went to a wedding last week—the bride in a cloth of gold sari & the groom in heavily embroidered jacket, jodhpurs and turban. It cdn't have been more delightful.

Every late afternoon, we go for a walk in the university gardens with A in his pram—all the herbaceous Eng flowers are looking lovely. In our garden, we have lupins, marigolds, cornflowers, sweet William and roses … and are eating our own veg.

Mama, if your new boss objects to your time-off for India, tell him what to do w his ledgers! For our sake and the baby's, please have all your injections, espy typhoid and cholera—do what the old quack tells you!

Tried on my posh dresses the other day, & can't get into any of them—isn't it ghastly! Actually, I only weigh 8.12, but the thin bits seem to be in the wrong places.

Delhi, Feb 25, 1965

Lots of sea-mail lost, ours & other peoples … How India will mend, I do not know, no one can trust anyone in official circles.

Gathered some nice twigs from the Ridge, including catkins wh reminded us of England. Our next-door neighbours have given us several gorgeous bunches of sweet peas.

O, Mummy, I just can't tell you how <u>beautiful</u> Aidan is—like a little cherub—he seems too good for earth … too good to be true. We shall have to look after him v carefully. I don't get more used to having him, but more and more amazed at his prettiness.

Went to the doctors today and now have a clean bill of health, so I feel v relieved. I now weigh 9.1, and must start to let out my summer clothes.

On Sunday, we are going to a hospital tea party

Papa, please send a photo of your telescope. It sounds fab.

We expect A's godmother to tea tomorrow. Now that I am home permanently, I intend to have a few tea parties.

Delhi, Mar. 6, 1965

Aidan (11.13) slept 11 1/2 hours last night—doesn't sleep much during the day—wd prefer to be played with all day—this morn, threw a toy out of the pram. He loathes having his face washed.

Evelyn Reading came & baby-sat so we cd go on the spree to N Delhi. We hadn't been since U Bill was here.

We haven't got 2 n.paise to rub together. we hope someone else is worrying how we shall get home & back for leave in 67.

How lovely to have snow. We pbby won't see any for years.

D will be away 3-4 days at Easter to take services at Jaipur—isn't it awful.

Delhi, March 8, 1965

Aidan … 2 more teeth.

We went to the Shakespeare director's party—Allan Sealy baby sat. I wore the black dress you gave me and it was a great success. There is another Shakespeare dinner in college, but it is too expensive so we won't be going.

We passed on your letters to Evelyn & Mrs. Sircar.

Y'day I bottled 6lbs of cape gooseberries & 3 lbs of apple pulp. We got extra sugar ration for Holi.

I have sent Cookie off early, so tonight we will have pea soup, salami sandwiches and apple pie & cream.

D has to go to Jaipur this weekend, but only away one night.

Delhi, March 18, 1965

10.45 a.m. My chores done, & Aidan is full, clean & asleep on the verandah. The pigeons are cooing & it is a lovely warm sunny day. The roses are blooming on the house walls & it is altogether rather pleasant.

Last Thursday, Sister Mary Earnshaw from the hospital came for tea and cuddled Aidan for hours!

Made a 2nd batch of homemade fudge, delicious though I say so myself—gave some to my neighbour, Mrs. Arya, and she passed over the hedge her home-made guava jelly.

Exams start in coll soon—D has to set some papers.

A is now sitting on my knee & sends lots of love to you both. He is very fond of displaying his big fat tummy by lifting up his dress. !! Think I'll take him round to the post for a walk and a change of scenery.

The Study, March 21, 1965

The feeding bottle teats arrived safely—thank you so much. The baby-book has failed to arrive, and the Jan. 'Housewife'.

On Monday, Fr Ernest John in for tea, on Tues, Fr. James Stuart to dinner, and Friday Fr. Dalaya.

We've just had that ghastly colour-throwing festival, Holi, but we managed to steer clear.

I hear return passages for you & D's mother have been booked. Re money, bring all you intend to use—banks here are consistently inefficient. Thanks for offering to bring cosmetics, but I hardly ever use them, but wish I did as the jars are so pretty.

The servants (though I hate that expression) are driving me nearly bats—they only half do jobs & make excuses for the other half.

We get quite a few poisonous spiders in the house and have to kill them—really, England seems such a mild, safe place to live!

Do you remember the little thistle-shaped vase you bought me years ago—I've got roses in it in the living room.

Delhi, March 27, 1965

Very pleased you wear the Nepalese hat we sent you, Papa. I keep seeing the most beautiful chess sets for you—I only wish we cd afford one. We must have some games when we are home.

Aidan 12.11 1/2 and eating carrots. He has 2 tremendous holes in his arm fm smallpox vaccination, but they are closing up, thank goodness. Going to sleep, he smiles & chuckles and is v funny to watch. Please send another pair of plastic pants. At 6.15 a.m. we woke to hear him talking like mad. He sounded so sweet. Please send another pair of plastic pants, no frills.

Made some lemon curd this afternoon. I haven't any appetite these days, and find it hard to think about food except in the lobster dream-world.

The sparrows are nesting everywhere. We've just thrown them out of the lampshade in the dining room, and now discover them behind the poetry books in the study!

I must write to Auntie Reta and Auntie Sylvia. Its fabulous about Kath's baby—it will be my niece or nephew!.

Delhi, April 6, 1965

We have lost loads of mail.

Aidan is such a happy, talkative baby. He doesn't like to be carried 'like a baby' but up on my shoulder he is happy.

We had a young Eng lecturer in for tea this week, and a local clergyman.

Helen Jerwood, one of the grand old ladies of Delhi has died—she was 85 & came to Delhi as a missionary when she was 25, and has founded 4 or 5 schools. She visited me in hospital, and Aidan held her finger. D & Evelyn went to the funeral.

Bottled some fruit this week.

We go to Simla 4th May to 12th July so we will miss 'the great sweat'.

Most of the flowers are finished now, but I can still pick fresh roses every day.

Delhi, Easter Day 1965

Very happy Easter Greetings. As I write, I am waiting for D to return from Jaipur ... he left on Thursday ... it has been a long three days.

I'm cooking a chicken for our Easter festival meal, and apple meringue—Cookie has today off—I painted some hard-boiled eggs.

Aidan has some prickly heat, but I'm keeping it in check. He is absolutely marvellous, holds his bottle with both hands ... wish you cd hear him laughing—loud & long.

The Nestle Baby Book has arrived, but it is old-fashioned nonsense—it regards all babies as machines. Think I'll write and tell them so!!

Temp now 95—we have not yet used fans ... rained today, dust storm y'day.

Last Wed, some friends we made on the ship came from Pakistan & brought us a bag of flour, bag of sugar, & some Black Magic chocs. Wasn't it terribly kind of them?

Delhi, April 9, 1965

Dear Papa ... advice please—varnish on the oil painting you finished just before we set off has come unset in this climate .... V pleased at your book news, hope it sells well.

Aidan is bouncing & sends his love.

SO looking forward to the mothers' coming in September. I know you say you are 'not an eating man', Papa, but you must promise to eat properly whilst Mama is away.

Delhi, April 14, 1965

SOS for Dinky feeders & plastic pants (no frills).

D is going to Jaipur.Thursday to Sunday,night, so the boy will be in my care alone!

Prospect Lodge, Simla, May 6, 1965

Reasons for delay in writing:-

25 Apr - a friend from Kerala for b'fast—2 friends for dinner,
26th - clergy friend for tea, Sircars for coffee after dinner,
27th - to the Son et Lumiere at the Red Fort, most enjoyable,
28th - to a dinner party at the Sircars to say goodbye to retiring head of St Stephen's Community,
30th - Evelyn Reading for tea & supper,
1st - an Australian who studied at Cuddesdon *[D's theological college]* for lunch & tea,
2nd - temporary railway colleague of D's father in UK, Mr Kamath of Madras & 3 boys for lunch.
4th May - left Delhi for here—I don't know how we ever got packed.

We had a v comfortable 2-berth sleeper from Delhi to Kalka 10.10 p.m.—7 a.m., and came up from Kalka by taxi, arriving Simla 11 a.m. The baby was an absolute model … he was actually looking out of the window during the last part of the journey. He is so happy, laughs and talks all day—now looking very beautiful asleep in his sleeping bag.

Lots of delightful scenes from the train in the morning— oxen threshing, camels turning grinding stones, a caravan of camels, village women with pots on their heads walking through the fields, all sorts of lovely glimpses of India.

Aidan can now actually propel himself in a worm-like way. He gets furious when he realises it is not quite right, and buries his head in his hands and howls v pathetically. He now eats stew minus meat … etc … 3lbs of milk every day—he is 14lbs 1oz. I don't want him to grow up, just be a Peter Pan, he's so cuddly! We've brought the pram to Simla, but it is awful pushing it up the hill, though D does the pushing. As I write, a terrific storm pounding like fury on the tin roof.

Simla, May 13, 1965

It is lovely to be out of hot Delhi, but it has been bitterly cold—3 sweaters not too many … after the rain, we can smell the pines … monkeys jumping on the roof, ugly, mangey beasts—I threw stones at some who kept waking up the baby.

The ADVENTURE *[2 mothers' visit]* we have arranged for Mrs. Ross to meet and shepherd you in Bombay … please bring 2 pots Marmite [etc, etc].

I'm having a great Bronte phase … Hoping to have a pair of handmade shoes made by a Chinese shoemaker, when holiday bills are paid …. Pat & Roger Hooker are coming to Simla to see us. *[he was fellow-curate of D in Stockton]*

Aidan has wonderfully rosy cheeks, & is looking v well.

Simla, May 23, 1965

… just like an English summer, torrential rain & thunderstorms. As I write, I can hear hail bouncing on the tin roof.

D is writing a sermon for Christ Church on the Mall, and Aidan is fast asleep (he absolutely adores custard & banana—15 lbs, 8 oz)

Simla, May 30, 1965

I am sitting in the sun, which is glorious w a background of dark green pines & a vivid blue sky, no monkeys in sight, and the birds singing merrily. Aidan has got lovely brown legs.

D and I both went to the dentist, highly qualified and well recommended. There is also a pavement dentist in the bazaar!

On Friday, we went out to lunch, all 3 of us, at Bishop Cotton School, a long though v beautiful walk, 2,000 feet down! Loads of wild flowers and berries, & some new birds.

Met Jane and Maqbul Caleb—he is chaplain, was a St. Stephen's student.

Many beautiful old books to be had here—D got a lovely early Coleridge ed., and I The Englishman's Country, full of beautiful old paintings & engravings.

Hired bikes for a fabulous ride with New Zealand friends to Mashobra, eternal snows in the distance, leaving Aidan with one of his Irish-missionary aunties. We took a picnic, but later stopped a man carrying a tin trunk on his head, a seller of biscuits and cakes.

Please send news of St.Peter's and parish magazines—we did enjoy the last lot.

Simla, June 6, 1965

We've been on a rather futile fishing expedition, a walk through wonderful country, but the river was nearly dry. At one point, we came upon a little temple, with holy man and a spring, where we refreshed ourselves—he gave us a pinch of sugar each.
On the way back, a road engineer gave us a lift in his jeep. A was looked after by one of his Irish aunties. He is definitely teething.

I have had injections & pills for dermatitis—rash was all over me but now almost disappeared … A v gd doctor here, so do not worry.

[long list of things for the mothers to bring—mostly foodstuffs, baby clothes]

My new Chinese shoes fit beautifully—they are a bit 'Auntie Reta'. *[the most fashionable of her aunts]*

Simla, June 20, 1965

[Juliet's mother had asked if we wanted them to bring anything 'frivolous'] Sorry to disappoint you, but we don't crave anything. D has asked his mother to bring him a new pair of sandals. & I am asking you to bring me a pleated white skirt —like the sort Auntie Reta bought for herself—in fact, that would do if she is thinking of throwing it out … also a couple of tins of kippers. Please bring my specs, and a set of 4 knitting needles and a good sock pattern. When you arrive, it will be like Christmas Days at once!

Sorry this is a rather 'gimme' letter. How are the stars, Pa? Please write soon and tell us of your astronomical adventures.

Simla, July 1, 1965

[List of things to bring] for my only youngish friend.

I have a deep abscess on my hip from a dirty needle when I was having dermatitis injections 4 weeks ago— spending a small fortune at a 2nd doctor, but the 1st will have to foot the bill!

Aidan is just wonderful, full of energy & giggles.

Going home on the 5th.

Delhi, July 11, 1965

What a difference it makes to be home—I feel v happy. The situation in the house at Simla was really intolerable because of the old battleaxe who ran the place *[English widow of Indian archdeacon]*.

Aidan is teething like mad and talking like mad. At the moment he has his legs over the pram side and is laughing and shouting down a Smartie tube.

I've lost a terrific amount of weight during the hols (a stone—now 8.5) so all my old clothes will probably fit again (damn it). Here are my statistics, though there's nothing v vital about them …

I was able to go to early church on St. Peter's day—D stayed w Aidan to let me go.

Terribly excited about September.

Delhi, July 15, 1965

Y'day. went about abscess to St Stephen's Hospital. To my great surprise, the doctor gave me a general anaesthetic … I cd cheerfully murder the first Simla doctor. In England, we would sue him, but Indian justice isn't worth the trouble and it would take years.

Wonderful surprise—I can get into my going-away dress, and it is slack!

D is at the Christian staff retreat today. A is playing w a crinkly piece of paper, and singing to me.

Delhi, July 22, 1965

[lots of requests from friends for the mothers to bring things— clothes, kitchen equipt, car parts] ... your luggage will be quite extensive!

Aidan 16.11—doc says he hasn't gained enough but he is so terribly active, unlike fat Indian babies who just sit and grow. The doc says a lot of stupid things & I am not in the slightest perturbed. A is great fun, and, my goodness, what a 'character'.

... wonderful that Kath has a son, Matthew.

Wonderful that Daddy wants to give me a dress ... quite bright colours for the tropics. It's astounding what you can wear here.

Your garden sounds lovely, just when ours is bare. We can't plant anything until after the monsoon.

Delhi, July 28, 1965

This morning, D brought Aidan into our bed about 6.30 a.m., & he immediately scrambled over to sleeping me & pulled my hair & chewed my nose until I woke up, of course all the time squeaking with laughter. He can crawl now—we have lots of fun with him on the lawn & he can move at a terrific speed.

Delhi, August 3, 1965

POSITIVELY the last 'Bring' letter! You have no idea how grateful we are for all the things you are bringing. You'd think we lived in the outback, wouldn't you?!

... the Hookers are coming for a week.

Aidan is wonderful. At least, we think so. He is terribly advanced by my baby book.

Isn't it sad that Anchor Line is to finish—they really are v friendly ships

India, August 16, 1965

V pleased Mrs. Buxton rang you—she really is a rather odd cove *[to & fro in her Land Rover between foxhunting at home in UK, and in India helping in emergencies]*.

Your room is nearly ready—I have now made your bed-spreads, quilts etc.

Y'day we had a young English couple to tea—he is a manager at our bank, and y'day after dinner, 3 young lecturers dropped in for coffee—a pleasant evening ... they brought me some gorgeous water-colour paper, & I am doing a bit of painting—Indian folk, etc

India, August 27, 1965

Yes, do by all means borrow my watch—it is in the right-hand dressing-table drawer. It seems v strange to me to refer to possessions of mine elsewhere in the world!

Evelyn was here for tea & supper y'day, and today the friend with a little girl came to have her hair cut!

Aidan has a tiny corner of tooth peeping through. He loves his bath and splashes like mad.

[to Papa re his astronomy and painting]

India, Sept. 2, 1965

Dear Mama—No news—tell you when I see you!

Do sunbathe on deck, and enjoy the luscious food & service. Have a dip in the pool before b'fast. Come soon.

Papa will get his own letter in a day or two.

India, Sept 7, 1965

Dear Papa

[As the mothers set out from Liverpool by sea, an Indo-Pak war broke out, & we wondered how that might affect their plans]

From All India Radio, the BBC and the newspapers, we try to get some sort of picture, but it is very confusing. Amritsar on the border has been bombed but not heavily and Delhi has expected the same for the last two nights. We have a blackout at night, and no vehicles except a few buses are allowed. Y'day, we got in a supply of tinned foods in case there are shortages. Shops were packed with women buying 20 of this and a dozen of that … everyone is rather nervous. It may, however, blow over in a few weeks *[it did, before the mothers' ship reached Bombay]*. The danger is that this will be an excuse for the sort of communal rioting they had in 1947. We hear that the British in Lahore have been advised to leave, and a plane with women and children has already left.

Do not worry about us, because if it were considered necessary, we would all be flown home. It is a comfort to remember that when the Chinese invaded Assam, the British were moved out in 2 days ... have no fear ... we are all very well, and this morning is beautifully sunny and the gardeners are cutting the grass and digging over the flower beds.

On Sunday night, we went to bed late, and only half slept, straining our ears for noise from the sky above the sound of the fan. All was well, and last night also, so we wonder whether it is just a climax of suspense.

Thurs. Y'day evening, it was reported that some Pak paratroopers had been arrested carrying poison to put in the water tanks. We do not of course know how true this is. The college army cadets have organised patrols round the grounds throughout the night, and, as one patrol has HQ just outside our house, we feel rather more secure. Bombing we can do nothing about, but disguised paratroopers are rather scary. I have told you the truth as we know it, so that you will have an accurate picture because I do not want you to be worried for us.

Delhi, Sept. 17, 1965

Dear Papa, We assume that the mothers are on their way here.

We haven't had an air-raid for ages, and, when we did, it was a bit of a false alarm … we sleep through most sirens. Many of our boys are concerned w transporting wounded troops from trains to hospitals … There is a captured tank on display in the middle of Delhi, & it really is rather exciting, BUT also depressing. I do not mind bombing so much as the responsibility for Aidan, and the possibility of losing my home. Let's just hope that a little good sense will wriggle to the surface on both sides.

Some friends from Stockton have arrived for a week— they are terribly nice & really good company, esp for me.

The day after they leave, the whole house will be whitewashed in preparation for the mothers, and then you won't see me for polish & dusters.

Some men are building a trellis on the verandah to give the mothers some privacy and Aidan a huge playpen, an enormous cage.

The house [Stockton] must seem considerably larger now that all the things Mama is bringing have been removed! How are your paintings progressing? Any new commissions? Hope you have good skies this winter for astronomy.

I have designed and supervised the making of costumes for a college production of 'As You Like It'—seems a bit frivolous now, with a war going on!

England seems such a safe and homely place!

Delhi, Sept. 28, 1965

Dear Papa. Do not worry at all about the situation here —we are perfectly well & safe & cheerful, espy now the blackout is lifted.

Mama says they will stay longer in Aden to delay the ship's arrival … house whitewashed, the bedspreads are ironed and the floors gleaming—in fact, we are all set.

On Friday evening, D will go to the station to meet the mothers, & I will welcome them here.

[IndoPak conflict] a v devious case of aggression agst India … hasn't Wilson *[UK PM]* made a terrible boob? For goodness sake, why doesn't someone tell him.

Aidan eats what we eat, and drinks gallons of milk & just about wears us out each day. Rhyme, when he's being intolerable:
> Horror, horror in the pram,
> Who do you jolly well think you am.
He's a pet, but sometimes ghastly, too!

Delhi, October 9, 1965

[arrival of J's and D's mothers—Juliet's letters for the next few months were addressed to her father only as he stayed in Stockton while they visited us, sailing to and from India by Anchor Line]

Dear Papa

The dress you sent is absolutely marvellous … fabulous … unpacking the most terrific booty. When the mothers unpacked, it looked like the Customs shed—as you said, everything but the kitchen sink!

The maths books look <u>awfully nice</u>!. As soon as I have finished the cardigan I am knitting for Aidan, I shall get down to some sums

Today, the mothers and we went to a garden party, a v homely affair & we enjoyed it v much

Aidan is just lapping up all this grandmother business, & getting rather conscious of his effect on them. Some days, he lays it on thick, and, boy, do they love it !

Delhi, Dec. 20, 1965

Dear Papa

We all hope you have a Happy Christmas & a Scottish New Year in Edinburgh.

I expect Mama has kept you informed of all our doings … very pleased you enjoyed A's painting, his third—I think Father Christmas is putting crayons in his stocking.

I am in the process of icing the cake, & on Thursday will bake a batch of mince pies …. the chicken is ordered. We shall even have holly (from Simla) Do get a bit of greenery for the old house.

Doing costumes for a modern play, 'Rhinoceros'.

Aidan is thriving and this cold weather has given him rosy chccks ... 6 tccth.

[Juliet did not write to her father often, as her mother wrote to him regularly]

* * * * *

INTERLUDE 'Sisters'

[This is a piece that Juliet wrote, referring to our friends and neighbours of the Anglican women's St. Stephen's Community. Although she fictionalised the account, there is no mistaking the community, or the story told here, and Juliet's reflections provide a deeply perceptive, sympathetic and realistic picture]

It wasn't until after the baby was born that Vera realised how badly she had let the side down. Everyone was delighted with the baby and the fact that there was a missionary family again after more than twenty years with only single people on the station, but there was also an undercurrent of another feeling. It was hard to put one's finger on it exactly, but Vera sensed a slight air of disapproval when she visited the mission Community House.

A visit to the Community House was like stepping back half a century—charming, but definitely antique. If it were teatime, tea, toast and biscuits would be served, the teapot being topped up from an ornate silver spirit kettle. On her first visit, Vera had time, as she sipped her tea, to observe her surroundings while her husband talked to the head of the sisterhood.

The ceiling of the main room was very high and in the gloomy corners birds had nested on the beams. Black blinds covered the upper windows, and the lower ones were shaded by the wide verandahs outside. Victorian furniture with dust-collecting knobs and ledges was ranged round the grubby, yellow-covered walls. Some of the chairs had faded cotton covers that had been smart thirty years before. Small, darkly polished tables were set beside the chairs and in the window alcove someone had made an attempt to brighten these dowdy surroundings by putting a jug of sun-shiny marigolds on a small native carved stand.

At one end of the room was a large glass-fronted book-case full of books with faded spines. In the absence of any new books, the old ones seemed enshrined in their useless-ness.. Next was an old piano with an embroidered runner on top. A few faded, brown-mottled photographs com-pleted the decorations.

At the other end of the room, behind her chair, Vera could just glimpse the long, shining dining table through the half-opened door. A small brass bell was its only ornament, and that, she learned later, was for summoning servants.

It was nice to be invited to tea, and she would try and become friends with the pale, tired-looking members of the mission, one of whom she had first seen when she came to greet her and her husband off the overnight train. Vera would try hard not to regard these people as misfits but as dedicated, yet it was hard when all of them seemed to have some peculiarity that had perhaps pushed them out of western society and into an area where they could build their lives again. Perhaps that mentally poised question mark was the first moment when she sensed a slight hostil-ity.; a slight distancing hardly acknowledged by those re-sponsible for it.

When the visit was over, Vera hardly knew whether she was pleased to be thought a suitable candidate for inclusion. As she walked with her husband back to their bungalow, Vera wondered if he had noticed how odd the Community House was.

Later, when her husband was in his study, Vera sat on the verandah of the half-furnished bungalow listening to the crickets and enjoying the scent of jasmine on the slight breeze. Dreamily she recalled the tea-party and the sisters, who would be her nearest British neighbours.

Mary was tall, with mousey hair and a nervous tic. The white uniform dress of the mission made her seem paler than she really was , and her faded brown eyes belied her apparent vitality at tea.

Helen was also very tall, with long feet and boney hands. She wore mens' sandals and a man's watch. The uniform suited her well, and for all her largeness she seemed to have a more realistic and sympathetic approach to the weaknesses and failings of others.

Beside her sat Patsy, who, it seemed to Vera, had long ago renounced everything that could enhance her delicate skin and fine bones. She had faded to a thin shadow with a pale voice and an anxious expression. Patsy's eyes were like deep brown berries, but the overhanging eyebrows made them seem like those of a frightened mouse peeping out at the world. She was only a visitor, from up-country, resting from her labours in 'the field', 'The field' was an expression Vera would hear often, and soon learned that it referred to any missionary endeavour among the natives.

By contrast with Patsy, there had been a plump, curly-haired lady at the party. It seemed to Vera that she was almost normal, until she spoke, or, rather, laughed. It was the extended nervous laughing that Vera had heard from elderly bachelor clergy when they were in a group that included women. How had this pretty woman become so alienated from the world. She seemed so sparkly and interesting and had a genuine enthusiasm for the responsibilities she had for the hostel she ran at a remote school. Yet somehow she had lost hold of a vital ingredient of normality.

However odd all these women were, Vera had to remind herself that they were all dedicated workers in the fields they had chosen, and all convinced of their vocation.

Alice had been the mission member who had made the biggest impression on Vera. Alice was pretty and rosy-cheeked, not having been out long enough to have lost her healthy good looks and taken on the tired pallor of her companions. She was young and lively as she passed round tea and attempted small talk to fill in the awkward gaps in the conversation. She seemed trying to apologise for her fellow mission members.

Vera wondered what unhappiness had driven Alice to leave her nursing job in England and join these strange companions. Of course, she could not have known that her service in this far-off country would involve her in such a bizarre domestic situation.

Vera was pleased and a little surprised to see that Alice had polished nails and wore a ring on her finger, the only piece of jewellery among the Community House family. Seeing this evidence of an attempt to be serious-minded and attractive, Vera was slightly reassured, and her own position seemed less conspicuous.

During the following months, Vera often visited the Community House, and began to get some understanding of the calm centre which linked the mission members and made them a supportive family. Vera's own duties included teaching in the mission school as well as supporting her husband's work. They lived a Spartan life with little but the bare necessities of furniture, a few favourite pictures brought with them, and the books needed for their work. Food, too, was sparse, and, though well-cooked, often insufficient. As the months went by, Vera and her husband lost a great deal of weight, and, with it, the pink bloom from their faces. Soon they looked more like the other mission members and less like the tourists they sometimes encountered in the city.

Sometimes, when Vera visited the Community House, she would gaze at the brown mottled photographs of earlier mission members, which hung on the pale washed walls. Rows of uniformed women with dedicated faces gazed back. Some had awkward long necks and protuberant

112

teeth; some had the odd look of people who live alone for long periods in isolated places. Occasionally, there would be a pretty face or a plump little figure in the front row. Vera tried to imagine the devotion behind all those godly women and what they had turned their backs on to come to this strange existence in a foreign, sometimes hostile country.

Perhaps it was for some escape from impossible pressures at home or unhappy love affairs. But most of them had that earnest, dedicated look of people treading a straight, difficult path because they cannot refuse the challenge.

It was the pretty, relaxed faces on the photographs that intrigued Vera most, and one day she was tempted to ask the mission family about some of their predecessors.

As she listened, Vera was able to reconstruct the past that had taken place in that faded sitting room. Names and incidents were recalled, and some of the rather fierce characters of some of the outstanding names made Vera shudder, although she also admired their single-minded earnestness in the face of some of the most restrictive traditions of their adopted country. Every now and then, Vera would point to one of the calmer, prettier faces, and a ripple of embarrassment would go round the tea table. A slight pause, a whisper of discomfort and disapproval, "Oh, she did not last very long" or "She was only here a short time" and other vague remarks were made until it seemed rude to pursue the topic further.

It was interesting to Vera that Alice seemed to listen as carefully as she herself, and seemed equally dissatisfied with the unresolved explanations for the departure of certain members.

Vera was to learn later that one or two had gone home and got married. Others could not fit in with the mission rules, or found the rigours of the climate too exhausting. One had, Vera learnt much, much later, eloped with a young bachelor member of an adjoining mission. Another had committed the ultimate indiscretion of having an affair with a native.

About a year after this particular visit to the Community House, Vera was sitting on the hospital verandah listening to the noises of the city about her. Her baby lay in the tiny crib in her room and she was enjoying the cool air, thinking over the past day before retiring for the night. So many mission members had been to see them, and some had brought guests from up-country. One very old, very erect lady, with grey hair swept back into a severe bun, had come to see her, and Vera had put her finger into the tight grip of the baby's small hand. The old lady was almost blind. She had devoted her long life to her adopted country, but Vera saw that stern expression soften as the baby's gentle skin touched the large, gnarled, sunburnt hand.

It was then that Vera realised why other mission members, although kind and friendly, had seemed to distance themselves from her as her pregnancy advanced. The old lady, for all her authoritative bearing, had lived long enough and had enough experience of human nature and the natural order of life to be able to share the joy of a new life. She seemed to convey her understanding of family life, too, and of the love that surrounded the baby.

Vera thought that the other sisters felt uncomfortable because of her closeness to a member of the opposite sex and her reluctance to participate in mission activities that would disrupt her life with her husband. The baby was proof of the ultimate indiscretion and weakness, and that she had been almost selfish in having a special, warm and safe understanding with another person instead of having to feed on the community's love and understanding.

Only Alice seemed as friendly as before, and she herself was soon to become one of the members no one talked of any more, for Alice had shared her secret with Vera. She was engaged to be married to a native.

This pretty girl, more normal than any of the other women in the mission community, was about to be sent into the wilderness. The Community House family were all dedicated to the ideas and the ideals of the past, and unable to take that leap of faith to a possible new order of understanding. It made them sad, but they were quite unable to see their sister as anything other than a traitor. Alice would find that her former mission family would be beyond her reach, and the new culture she was to find a place in would always regard her as a stranger.

Vera hoped that Alice was as strong as some of those doughty characters in the old photographs, for she would need all of her resources to be happy in her unexpected choice of life.

* * * * *

1966 TEACHER OF ART AND CRAFTS

Delhi, March 1, 1966

Dear Papa *[mothers homeward bound]*

It is quite strange not to call The Mothers to meals, but no doubt they are enjoying themselves immensely with the Anchor Line.

The 'As You Like It' sweat is over, but I am now working on costumes for the High Commission play. 'Cranford' … am also catching up on all my needlework … I am trying some maths, too.

Aidan is flourishing and up to constant mischief … I will post this when we go for our morning walk … I was interested to see your astronomy articles.

Delhi, March 10, 1966

Dear Papa. Well, Mama must soon be home, and how excited you must feel to see her and to hear first-hand all the adventures. I think tomorrow they will be in Gibraltar I think they hoped to visit Malta also.

A is full of mischief, and just when he is due a spank, he comes & flings his arms round my neck and delivers a big kiss, so really he just twists me round his little finger. He is becoming a naughty mimic. I am furiously knitting and sewing for him.

I am also busy designing clothes for a fashion parade in New Delhi which a college boy and I are organising. I can't get my ideas down fast enough.

[Juliet worked at this sort of thing with two gifted students, Martand Singh and Rajee Sethi. They both became world-figures in regard to textiles and design]

I am sending home the little painting that you did, to renovate—I shall collect it in a year's time!

Could you possibly check out my bike for me, and ensure it is not going too rusty.

Well, Papa, you had better get the flags & bunting ready and order the band for the wanderer's return! Fondest love.

Delhi, April 1966

[Juliet wrote this and the next letter to her mother on the homeward voyage]

Dear Mama, At the moment, I am sitting at the nursery table, and Aidan is howling because I won't give him the pen. He really has grown since you left. He is now sitting on my knee & has stopped howling.

Do tell Papa I am studying the mathematics almost daily, & v much enjoying it! *['The' mathematics—Juliet and her anti-quarian-bookseller father enjoyed this antique style]*

The roses on the house walls have been magnificent— the pink and red striped ones & yellow & peachy ones, all out together.

Molly Heard *[High Commission]* is coming to dinner next week.

Evelyn babysat, so we could get to the High Commission's 'Cranford'. My name was in the Statesman and Times of India for the costumes.

I made palm crosses from the little tree by the vestry door for our Palm Sunday service, and helped D rearrange the chapel for the Maundy Thursday eucharist.

The temp is now up to 100—Aidan has discarded his shirt and likes to sit on my knee & look at pictures … we had a nice evening walk with him round the university gardens

Evelyn was here the other day & brought a bubble-blowing set for A.

I am knitting and sewing like mad, & have borrowed Elspeth's sewing machine ….
Unfortunately, I am reading the last of the Bronte books & have read all George Eliot and J Austen, and am going to start on Dickens next. At the moment, I have on the go the Bronte, and books on archaeology, mountaineering and genetics.

I made some pickled onions the other day, & today tomato pickle.

Delhi, April 18, 1966

Dear Mama We had a lovely dinner party with Molly Heard, with first and last courses on the sitting-room verandah. We are all going to tea with her on Sunday.

Temp 101 today … Have made tomato juice from our vast tom crop.

Aidan is a great dancer and singer to Indian music. D managed very well putting him to bed when I went to Cranford rehearsal.

D had a v interesting Easter round in Rajasthan, and we managed v well at home, with Babu Lal staying for security.

We have sacked Ram Piari (sweeper) for stealing, and now have a v nice, reliable whirlwind.

Delhi, May 2, 1966

Dear Mama & Papa … I'm rather bothered with asthma —the neem is flowering, a common irritant, so do not worry.

Evelyn baby-sat so that we cd go to the new Bishop's institution and on to the Queen's Birthday celebration at the High Commissioner's residence. Swallowing my anti-royalist leanings with the 'wee droppe', I enjoyed the evening, and my goodness it was interesting anthropologically ! We were announced and swept forward to meet Freeman [*John Freeman, UK High Commissioner*], & then bang slap into Rimington [*another diplomat, whom the mothers had met on their outward ship, married to Stella*]. Actually, he seemed quite nice, & his performance in 'Cranford' was magnif. We did meet some awfully nice folk, & observed some interesting ones.

24th - To Molly Heard's for tea (she sends her regards to you). It is a lovely flat, but I think much more cd be done with it.

29th - a young friend in for coffee. We went to the Cranford cast party & had a lovely supper & liquid refreshment, but most people were rather non-friendly as we're not diplomatic …. Allan Privett & Cookie shared the baby sitting.

30th - out to coffee at the bank manager's wife's, & at night a student in to dinner.

2nd - the Groves, a new family, in for tea—we all got on extremely well.

Dresses given by Evelyn and Elspet] have solved a few problems with bills, I can tell you.

Delhi, May 11, 1966

Having sweated through 114 and a dust storm, we are now rather cooler, having had torrential rain … the garden looks fresh and there is a lovely cool smell.

D is away marking exam papers 7 a.m.-2 p.m. this week, & is tutoring a princess, the daughter of the Maharaja of Dewas Junior, and niece of the Mah of Jaipur & the Mah of Cooch Behar—the head of the princess's school at Jaipur wrote to ask D—he is working v hard for our holiday.

A now insists on eating his lunch w a fork & feeds himself entirely except for the odd lot I pop in to speed the process. The carpenter has just delivered some beautiful teak building bricks, all sorts of shapes. I designed them to be useful for A learning geometry etc later. I am now busy with his alphabet book and some pictures.

Had a friend to dinner last night, and tonight it is Allan Privett's last, it will be a 'real Punjabi blow-out'!

The leeks are growing quite big, and we've planted a creeper in the sweetpea trellis.

Delhi, May 16, 1966

7.45 a.m. D & Brijraj have gone off to their examining stint—Brijraj has b'fast here these mornings & it is a v jolly affair.

On Sat, a shopping spree to New Delhi, and we took A into Standards Restaurant for lunch. He behaved v well, & enjoyed fish and chips with spinach, & ice cream. The waiters were rather tickled.

This morning we are going to coffee with Mrs. Howatson (Bank wife), so A will have a playmate.

I am so sorry to hear that Poppa *[maternal grandfather]* is not well—poor frail little Nana all alone. I was thrilled to have a letter from them

B Lal was away 4 days and we managed v well … he really is ageing and I shall be glad when we no longer require him … D enjoys my cooking, too!

I have cut off my long hair & returned to my old hairstyle—urchin/Brutus.

We have today acquired a darling little pussy cat. He is supposed to be Siamese, but I hope he's not got ambitions, because at the moment he looks as if he will be plain marmalade. A is thrilled to bits, & the kitten follows him about. The kitten is only 1 month old, far too young to leave his Mummy, but he can lap milk and use his sand tray. He has a gorgeous purr.

* * * * *

c/o de la Hoyde, St. Nicholas Parsonage, Nain Tal, U.P. June 3, 1966

[Before we move on to Juliet's first letter from our short Naini Tal holiday, here is a piece she wrote about the journey there from Delhi]

Our holiday began at two thirty in the morning, and we spent the first half hour listening to the crickets and waiting for the taxi to arrive. Eventually we heard it wheezing and spluttering along the road and recognised it by its single working headlamp. Ram Singh looked sleepy, his turban a little askew, and a thick cotton shawl draped around his shoulders. His companion, similarly draped and sleepy, had come along to hold two wires under the dashboard and so enable the expedition to start. We loaded our cases, bedding rolls and pushchair into the open boot and said goodbye to Delhi and the hot weather.

At the bus station, which, surprisingly, we reached unscathed, all was noise and bustle. Round the lights above the depot, buzzed and dived hundreds of small insects. It was best to wait in the dark and hope to be missed by the cruising mosquitoes.

A number of buses were loading up goods and passengers. Our luggage was hauled onto the roof of ours, and we carried on board a bag of essentials for the journey and a large clay water pot woven round with rope. Filled to the brim, some of the water in the pot would gradually soak through the clay, and, as it evaporated, would keep the remaining water in the pot cool. In the bag was a flannel and soap, a fruit knife, books, sunglasses and scarves for our faces in case of a dust storm. Our seats, a long padded bench immediately behind the driver, were called 'upper class', and behind us was a half-division, and beyond that, less well-padded seats known as 'lower class'.

There seemed to be plenty of room for everyone and their luggage. We were all very cheerful although it was virtually the middle of the night, and, by the time the bus shuddered into life, had all greeted one another. Foreign travellers in India must accustom themselves to answering personal questions such as details of family, work and salary from other passengers. This is not regarded as impertinence but as a way of establishing friendly contact.

The journey became hotter and dustier as the morning wore on and we were glad of our pot of water. Along the trunk-road we hurtled at an alarming speed and could hardly hear ourselves think above the noise of the engine, Every now and then, we would see by the roadside a huge lorry on its side.—evidence of a gamble that had not paid off. The general idea was for vehicles from both directions to hug the crown of the road with horns blaring, each expecting the other to give way. It was in fact just possible for two large trucks to pass with care, but often the manoeuvre was left until it was too late. There seemed, however, to be few casualties and it was all regarded as part of the adventure of travel.

We were relieved to reach our first stop intact. All the passengers left the bus and made for the nearest tea stall.

This was an open-sided stall covered with a piece of red canvas and heaped with small sun-baked clay pots. These were filled with very hot ,sweet, stewed tea, cooked with the milk, and it tasted surprisingly good on a hot, dusty throat. The extreme sweetness, which would normally have revolted me, was quite acceptable, and a quick way of producing the energy needed to cope with the rigours of the journey. The handle-less pots lasted long enough for us to enjoy the drink, and then we, with all the other customers, smashed them on the floor. This was usual at railway stations too, and ensured everyone got a clean cup, and did away with the complicated caste requirements regarding washing up and untouchability.

Before we remounted our seats behind the driver, our fair-haired, blue-eyed baby was admired and had his cheeks pinched in the best Indian style of doing 'baby puja' or baby worship. He rose to the occasion with big smiles and we all got back on the bus with the feeling of a big family outing.

The driver continued with his suicidal style of driving and by some miracle, after many dusty, noisy miles, the ground began to rise and we reached the green foothills. Here we had another halt, while the driver went to pay the road toll, and the bus was surrounded by young boys selling small baskets of fruit and leaf-bags full of savoury snacks. We bought the first strawberries we had seen for nearly three years. Small and sweet, more like the wild strawberries of Britain, they tasted wonderful.

It was almost three in the afternoon, and about the time when normally we would be feeling at our most sleepy, but here there was a cool breeze and unbelievable green. I spent only a moment imagining how our tired driver was going to negotiate the hairpin bends on the road ahead, another moment considering the precipitous drop over the edge of the road, but then decided that, since I was not driving, I might as well relax and enjoy the scenery—it might be my last opportunity!

After ten minutes of twists and turns, we had lost our sense of direction, while the thick forest ahead gave no clue as to where the road was going next. We could soon smell the pine trees, and the air had a tingling edge to it, like an early morning at the end of a British summer. The skies were blue, with white clouds carrying blessed showers, instead of the yellow haze of sand-laden air we had endured for weeks in Delhi. The views were breathtaking, and we craned our necks for the first glimpse of the eternal snows.

Another two hours elapsed before we caught a fleeting glimpse of the far mountains as the clouds parted for a moment to reveal them. We had hardly time to gasp before we were flung round another bend and plunged again into the forest.

Eventually, we lost a little height, and cruised slowly between the outlying huts of Naini Tal. Soon, we were at the bus stop and saying goodbye to our new friends on the bus.

Coolies surrounded us, and we soon retrieved our luggage from the assortment being lowered from the bus roof. Suitcases were loaded onto the head of one coolie, and another carried the bedding rolls and the various small items …. We were greeted by our rosy-cheeked friends. Their good health was in a strange contrast to our yellow-tinged pallor.

It was strange to see rooms with fully upholstered furniture after our hot-weather cane furniture in Delhi, and to see ceilings uncluttered by fans. Our clothes were filthy and our skin felt gritty after the dusty bus ride, but we were soon revived by tea, seemingly almost the whole world's answer to exhaustion, and hot baths.

How much more must such a welcome have been appreciated in the old days after perhaps a week of travel in very much less comfortable conditions. 'Naughty Naini' was the old nickname for this hill station, for it was the place where young officers on leave and young ladies hoping for a husband could relax after the formalities of official life on the plains.

After dinner, we went to bed early, with the comforting feeling of blankets and quilts and the knowledge that in the morning it would be cool and invigorating.

* * * * *

Dear Mama and Papa,

Well, we are on our holidays. On Wed.1st June, we got up at 2 a.m., got a taxi at 3 to catch a bus to Naini Tal at 4. The journey takes 11 hours, and it was v comfortable & we had plenty of water & sandwiches. There were several stops, but we only gpt out of the bus once. Aidan was v excited but v v good. The journey was rather monotonous until we started to climb through the mountains. The scenery then was fantastic, great craggy mountains and deep pine forests. At one stop, we bought fresh strawberries, our first taste of them since leaving England!

When we arrived in Naini, there was the usual ghastly rush of coolies for custom. We engaged several and a rickshaw for me & Aidan, & D walked—but they took us to the wrong parsonage at the far end of the lake. It happened however to be the home of the chief UP policeman. He insisted on giving us tea before sending us on in a police jeep!

The de la Hoyde's house is gorgeous, in the middle of the forest and within 3 mins. walk of a lovely view of the lake several hundred feet below … the house is geared to children. We get tremendous appetites, and there is plenty to eat—unlike Simla! A is v excited, playing with Rachel de la Hoyde (she's 2) and it is a joy to see him so obviously enjoying his holiday.

Naini Tal, June 1966

This morning—joy of joys—I went for a long horse ride —it was lovely to be back in the saddle for the first time since we came to India—in glorious country. D stayed at home with A, drawing.

The 'little monsoon' is here, scattered downpours & brilliant sunshine. We are right above the town, and engulfed in swirling clouds a lot of the time. We have had a fire in our room to dry our clothes. A. had his first pony ride this morning. He is looking like a farmer's lad in Wellingtons & that yellow jersey you started.

There are lovely, long-tailed, silver monkeys around the house, and this is leopard & panther country!

Last week we went for a picnic by a river, & all bathed & fished & had a glorious time. A. now has a cricket bat!

Delhi, July 14, 1966

[we returned from Naini Tal on 7th July]

I am revelling in the heat (84-106) after the chill winds, swirling clouds, torrential rain and <u>hail</u> of Naini Tal.

Babu Lal and Jumia have completely scoured the house, so it was a very sparkling homecoming.

Aidan is missing Rachel's company, but is finding plenty of tricks of his own—I left him in the garden playing with the hosepipe, and the next thing I knew, the sitting room was flooded, and he looked v pleased with himself ... He is mango mad.

A new issue of 'Housewife' today—it is lovely. They are coming regularly.

Yarm seems very near—the sunshine here reminds me of when I came on a pony to see you at your business there, Mama. I was riding 'Flash' and it was a sunny morning.

Term starts tomorrow. David Baker, our new colleague from Australia, & Brijraj have both called ... it seems strange that Allan Privett is not here. Evelyn has been to see us after her holiday in the south,

Delhi, July 31, 1966

I have just finished with A for the day & am having a break before making dinner.

... The other day, A & I went swimming with my friend Jean in a gorgeous pool at Maiden's Hotel—A loved it. We spend a whole day at each other's house alternate weeks.

I am going to be v busy in the future as I am starting social work amongst servants' wives in college. The bursar, Dr. Ghose, has agreed to allow me to have Rs.200 to provide the beginning of knitting and sewing classes, & I hope also to do some hygiene, childcare and, family planning work with them. I also have lots of ideas re the children … with a team of students from the Social Service League to help.

[This was a remarkable project in several ways—while students of the college were about to start going to Bihar in groups to help in the famine, Juliet had the vision & compassion to reach out to transform the lives of these women on our very doorstep—20 or 30 were involved and it was truly transformative for many of them. A revolutionary feature was that Juliet welcomed the entire group into our house for their classes—there was not another staff house in the college where this sort of hospitality to this lowly group would have been conceivable, and it is a measure of Juliet's character and conviction that it happened. Nothing I did in our time at St. Stephen's had this profound significance. At the same time (literally), as the paragraph below indicates, her art-and-craft interest and skill brought her into collaboration with the student, Rajeev Sethi, who was to become a world leader in art and design. We still have a beautiful large and characteristic painting of his in our house in Scotland].

I am also on the Fine Art Soc committee in college, and will organise similar exhibitions to the one we had when you were here. Perhaps I'll give some art lectures.

<u>Also</u> (!) Rajeev Sethi (that artistic boy) & I are organising our own fashion parade for New Delhi with the backing of several fabric firms, and have been asked to do a monthly fashion show in N Delhi. This is all for our designs, he does women & I do men

<u>Also</u>! I am designing some jewellery for a N Delhi firm.

So life will be full. Also am sewing & knitting like mad for A, and trying to get some reading done … Thackeray's 'Henry Esmond'

Am also doing quite a bit of baking, & managing to entertain quite a few people.

Lots of boys come to say hello at the beginning of term, & quite a few just drop in for a chat.

The weather is v enervating at the moment because of the humidity. The garden is shooting up at present, esp weeds. I had a session this evening and managed to clear quite a few.

A's appetite is enormous these days, and he has an egg every morn. & usually a proper supper / high tea! He loves to play in the rain, & tonight got covered in mud.

Evelyn comes on Tuesdays usually, & that enables D and me to go shopping in N Delhi.

Delhi, August 1966

I don't usually write again so soon, but the atmosphere this morn has prompted me to do so. It feels exactly like a Sunday morn at 37!! D has gone off to Sunday School, & there is a slightly cool breeze through the gentle warmth of the day. I can just hear a neighbour's radio & the occasional bus go past. The birds are singing, & the sky is bright white with a few grey clouds. Do you see the rememblance? A is playing in the garden with the sweeping brush and is getting very black and a good appetite for lunch.

Had a party for the 4 bachelors, Brijraj, David Gosling, Balbir Singh, Wm Crawley.

11th - morning coffee at Jean's ....

A couple of 'overlanders' from Huddersfield for dinner, very homely pair, steak & kidney pie & sultana pudding—he said "you 'it the jackpot!"

That afternoon, the first women's needlework class—they seem to be a success, & I have a v reliable and energetic Brahmin boy to help, Prem Prakash Sharma.

12th - helped with costumes for a drama competition ... Evelyn to dinner.

15th - Melitza & Taj Srivastava (going to Keele Univ for a year) came to dinner—we have bought their tricycle for A and he is thrilled.
Today, a college contemporary of D's, Geo Lunn , for lunch, then we went shopping while Evelyn baby sat.

Reading Shakespeare, as I have been asked to do sets & costumes. [The College standards were high, the annual Shakespeare production reported in the annual journal from Stratford]

Delhi, August 24, 1966

My dear Mama & Aunties Reta, Sylvia & Irene .... I hope you do not mind sharing this letter because it is such a family grief ... We were very shocked & saddened to receive your letter today, & our prayers are with you all... I cannot adequately express my affection for Poppa [J's maternal grandfather], & feel a very great loss at his passing. It was one of my dearest wishes that Aidan would meet him, but now I must be content to pass on some of the pride I felt in having such a fine man for a grandfather.

I know you will do what you can for little Nana ... the sudden breakage of such a long shared life *[she moved in with Juliet's parents]*

Delhi, Sept. 14, 1966

Last week we had Roger Hooker to stay overnight ... a Jain friend for supper—he loves our vegetarian cooking! and that day 2 friends from Kanpur called, and Aidan went for his first party which he thoroughly enjoyed.

Y'day, had a friend over for the day and talked & knitted.

On Tuesday, talks w Shakespeare Soc about sets I am designing for 'Comedy of Errors'.

Wed, Evelyn for lunch, and an SCM tea party at the house, Ruth Roseveare for dinner.

My knitting scheme is going quite well, and last Sat I bought lots of wool wholesale. The women are very keen, always calling at the house for advice, and I am now getting some knitting orders for them.

Just lately, A and I have been spreading rugs under the big tree & spending the day outside—much cooler than inside. Took Aidan to communion in chapel on St. Aidan's day. He now insists on sitting at the table, and has abandoned his high-chair, and even attempts to use knife and fork properly. He walks down to the office with us every evening now. He brought me a present of a worm the other day!

We went for a walk in the wind on the Ridge the other day as D had a holiday, and we found a mutiny grave—a Lt.Edwards from Plymouth, aged 27. A most touching inscription by his wife. It was only about 200 yards from the flagstaff, where he fell with 4 brother officers. A most interesting morning.

Evelyn is having a stall at St Thomas' bazaar and I am sewing like mad for it.

Wed - we are giving a young bachelor lecturer a birthday party.

Thurs. my class—none of them can read, so I am devising symbols to represent knitting instructions.

Friday, to Jean's for the day, and in the evening Mrs. and Fr. Dalaya to dinner.

Delhi, Oct. 9, 1966

[details of plans for homeward travel for next year's leave, via Holy Land, staying in Jerusalem and Nazareth—where we had supported a child while at St. Peter's— then Athens, and Switzerland with best man Paddy & Caroline Orr—I was arranging to teach while in UK— mission agency agreed to raise our pay to normal missionary level]

St. Thomas' fete, helping Evelyn with her stall (I made a fairy doll and a bride doll for it)—A&D had a good afternoon together—the new bishop's wife opened the event, and then gave Aidan her garland!

133

On Friday, went for our first picnic of the season, to the zoo—A's eyes nearly popped out of his head all day .... saw three white tiger cubs, gorgeous, with blue eyes. We passed the place where we had a picnic with you, and it did seem strange.

Jean buys groceries from Hong Kong—so we have a jar of Marmite & some prunes in the house (we pay her in rupees).

[rioting students—not our college] we expect more fun and games next Monday.

Delhi, Oct. 20, 1966

D left at lunchtime for an SCM camp at Chandigarh ... the house seems so awfully empty without him ... Cookie is sleeping in the little room, as he does if D is away.

I've been helping with the Union play, Durrenmatt's 'The Physicists' and this evening popped over to college for the first night.

Monday—Jennifer Thorpe from St. Stephen's Community came to dinner.

Wed. some folks for tea, and an old student for dinner.

D's mother is meeting Fr. Weathrall on Darlington station, on his way back to Delhi, to give him a parcel for us.

I've designed the sets for the Shakespeare production, 'Comedy of Errors', but not sure whether I'll be doing the costumes—that depends on The Queen! (Elspeth Shankland)

Aidan loves reading & singing, dancing & saying prayers! He can snap his fingers too, the little wretch! When he sees D coming, he runs to the gate shouting Daddy Daddy—Mummy, Daddy. He loves to pass things at the table, and he can undress, in a rather rough way. I've just finished two sweaters for him.

Today, we took him to the NCC parade for National Solidarity Day, and Kikum Sangtam, Best Cadet, remembered Mama from last year.

I'm writing a magazine for circulation among the servants' children. Students will put it into Hindi.

Delhi, Dec. 25 1966

On Friday, Evelyn babysat, & we went Christmas shopping—I bought D one of those fur hats, and he gave me a gorgeous black & turquoise shawl for evening wear—also a lovely wooden box made in the college woodwork room for jewels (tell Auntie Reta!)

We got A to hang up a stocking, & you shd have seen his face in the morning! Evelyn brought him a lovely stuffed toy cat etc. etc. We also gave him 2 new books—he loves books. Mrs. Sircar gave him a stuffed toy cowboy, and Jean a magic painting book.

D took the midnight mass at St. James, and A & I went with him to the 6.30 a.m. communion at the hospital. While D took communion to a patient, A and I went round some of the wards, including the nursery ward, where A loved all the little babies—then home, and D to St. James and then St. Thomas. Babu Lal and the sweeper came and garlanded us, and I cooked lunch—we had a Sikh friend, Balbir, for lunch. Then, this afternoon, the usual waifs & strays party—about 10 boys for a spot of home-baking. All v pleasant, but we feel rather tired now.

31st - Agra—we have come to visit Pat & Roger Hooker by the Taj Express, v comfortable but rather cold. Last night, thrill of thrills, 'the Aga Khan by moonlight' *[a joke told against an American tourist]*. Yes, we saw the Taj by moon-light, and it was out of this world.—rather earlier than the mob of tourists & it was absolutely silent in the silvery light —we wondered if you were looking at the moon, Papa … today, we saw Akbar's tomb … a v refreshing & pleasant few days. One of our college lecturers, Dwivs *[Prem Sagar Dwivedi]*, whose parents live in Agra, took us home for tea, and drove us round.

I must get busy with my new play and all the knitting and sewing that has to be done before April.

* * * * *

Delhi, Jan. 12, 1967

I am sitting on the verandah in the pale, chill sunshine—it really is very cold out of the sun.

Aidan is such a talkative chap these days and full of funny little ways and ideas. It is also interesting to watch memory developing.

On his second birthday (9th) … he said 'Happy Birthday Daddy' perfectly, sitting up in his cot and later serving us 'tea' from his tea-set … Evelyn came for tea, and later the Principal & Mrs. Sircar.

Y'day, Jean was here all day … Last night, very pleasant, dinner at St Stephen's Community.

Today, Roger Hooker is coming to lunch.

I must do some work on my Greek play tonight—this is Giraudoux's *Tiger at the Gates*, which will be performed at the college's Allnutt Gate, which we go through every day —a wonderfully imaginative way of doing the play. I might be involved in another one later in the month … knitting like fury.

Term has started more slowly than usual, but this is the long, hot term so there is plenty of news to come!

Delhi, Jan 25, 1967

Do you remember last year, Mummy, going to the Republic Day parade? Well, we are going again, tomorrow. We are so looking forward to it.

[next day] We had very good seats, thanks to General Rajwade again, and the whole parade was thrilling. A was espy thrilled with the camels & elephants … a fantastic display, well worth the dawn rising.

The de la Hoydes are in Delhi on holiday from Naini Tal, and this morning A and I went to the zoo w them in their car. We are all going for a picnic to Tughlaqabad on Tuesday.

We are due to arrive in UK on 4th May. At the moment we are trying to find out who will help us pay the fare!

Aidan has had croup, & I have slept in the nursery for 2 nights.

Someone gave him some paper flowers the other day, and he waters them regularly—his own idea. He is v good at handing things round at parties.

The nasturtiums look very pretty in pots around the verandah.

Thank you for 'Housewife' which arrived a week ago. Have just started Mrs. Gaskell's *Life of Charlotte B.*

Delhi, Feb. 7, 1967

The de la Hoydes are still in Delhi. We see them most days … went in their car for a picnic to Suraj Kund, the big ancient reservoir.

On Wednesday I went shopping with the producer for material for the latest play.

Thurs. a clergyman friend to lunch, the de la Hoydes to dinner—a nice candlelit meal together.

Friday, St. Stephen's won the cricket match against Hindu College, so we all had a holiday … There was a tragic death of a young Delhi clergyman, so we went to the funeral in the evening—Aidan was as good as gold in the packed church. The man left four tiny children & a wife who is quite uneducated, so unable to support the family … very sad indeed.

On Saturday we went to—wait for it—the ASHOKA HOTEL, guests of the Headlam-Morleys, friends of D's Mama. The poshest hotel in Delhi … super—I wore my new black dress, a present from Jean, and it was just right … the most fabulous treat for just one evening. They are terribly nice people.

On Sunday, D had to go to St. Thomas, so Denys de la Hoyde took chapel, and the family came to b'fast.

Went to a wedding reception this evening—D went to the wedding last night.

Tomorrow, a picnic at Buddha Jayanti garden with de la Hoydes.

Thurs - some folks to tea, Friday Evelyn will be here phew!

A's favourite occupations are painting, reading and his bike, and he adores helping with pastry. At night, he has a nursery supper, and then says 'Story, Mummy' and goes and stands by his cot to be lifted in. Five minutes & a story later, he is asleep. Couldn't be easier!

Delhi, 17 Feb. 17, 1967

D was offered a job on leave at University College, London but has just today got one at his old school, Darlington Grammar. Our plans are to make his mother's home at Darlington our weekday base, and Stockton our weekend holiday home. August & Sept will be a holiday—I'm already making out a shopping list!

I have just spent some birthday money on red chukka boots for Aidan—I told him they were for the holiday, so he said "Aeroplane shoes". He is v good at opening the door & letting boys into the study.

Delhi, Mar. 30, 1967

I did mean to write while D was away in Rajasthan at Easter, but I was too tired & Cookie has had loads of time off—his son, Hanson, is here at the moment, which will be a help for the next two weeks. We have decided Babu Lal must retire when we go on leave, but support for his family will continue through employing Hanson.

[UK arrival arrangements] We really do feel the need for a holiday, 4 years here at a stretch is long enough. We are both a bit thin, so please don't comment when we arrive! The last bit of the trip, with Caroline & Paddy, in Switzerland is meant to be a real rest with good food & mountain air and friends, and we have high hopes of its beneficial effect.

The Japanese student who tutored me in origami has just given me the most gorgeous little fan, & last night an African student, Fred Magezi, gave D a beautiful robe from Uganda. Aren't we lucky!

A continues to thrive, & talks his head off. According to the educationists, his vocabulary shd be 250 words, and is at least 490.

We leave Delhi by BOAC for Beirut at 8 a.m. on Friday, 14th, and shd be in Jerusalem by 5 p.m,. … north of England 4th May. We are all getting more & more excited.

St. George's Hostel, Jerusalem—Hashemite Kingdom of Jordan, April 15, 1967

'phew' … first port of call, and I am sitting up in bed with a hot water bottle & 3 blankets.

The day before the day before we left, we had a jolly bachelors' party, & they brought us a bottle of brandy. The day before, 42 people came to the house to say bon voyage. As we left, Babu Lal & Jumia garlanded us at 5.30 a.m., and the nightwatchman brought me a posy ... Nine people came to the airport ... more garlands.

The VC10 takeoff was just stupendous ... suddenly, the front tips up, rather like a horse rearing ... landed at Bahrein on the Persian Gulf for 40 minutes and some fresh air ... landing at Beirut we could see the blue Mediterranean and snow-covered mountains—a 3 hour wait so we had a second lunch ... Middle East Airways to Jerusalem, and we saw Mt Hermon with snow on top and Lake Galilee. By the time we got here, we had been travelling 18 hours, so we were jolly tired and slept 11 ours.

This morning, Mary North came from Nazareth to see us [from Stockton, working in St Margaret's Home for girls]. She showed us round ... the ancient pavement dating back to the time of Our Lord and possibly / probable the place of the arrest & condemnation ... I can't describe the thrill of this place ... Tomorrow, after communion in the Anglican Cathedral, we are going to Bethany, the Mount of Olives, Gethsemane, and the Kidron Valley in the morning. We called at a Russian Orthodox church, where the nuns were singing vespers. They found time in the middle of it to make a great fuss of Aidan. After lunch at an ex-student's house, we are going on the Via Dolorosa. On Monday morn we are to go to the Dead Sea, Bethlehem and the River Jordan. We could both of us cry with joy to be here. Aidan, apart from one or two moments, has behaved extraordinarily well. Poor thing is just longing to 'let rip', so we must plan our time most carefully. We cdnt be in a more comfortable place.

St. Margaret's Home, Nazareth, April 22, 1967

Well, now we are in Israel, and have seen so many wonderful things here in Nazareth.

Y'day we had a lovely picnic on the shore of Lake Galilee. We cdnt afford a taxi to go to Capernaum, so we had to miss that, but had a delightful quiet day watching the water and the fishing boats. We are travelling around in local buses, and it is v easy and v rewarding.

Our present accommodation is glorious, with views over the town & the surrounding hills. We have met Badira, the girl for whom D & I started the SPYPA scheme. It is cheering that she is still supported by St. Peter's young people

We are about to go and visit a carpenter in his little house—D met him by chance, and they invited us to visit them.

Sunday. Last night one of the St Margaret's Palestinian girls bathed Aidan and put him to bed. He made it very clear I was redundant! Today, he has been with the little ones all morning, and is at present having lunch with them. He calls them "Aidan's friends". I'm sure he will cry when we leave!

We had a lovely HC service this morning in the orphanage chapel. D is preaching in the parish church later this morning [the Arab vicar had trained at Bishop's College, Calcutta].We visited a convent where Charles de Foucauld lived in a little hut.

Monday—we are leaving A with the other children, and are going up Mount Tabor and to Cana with Miss Jones, the headmistress, and Badira.

On Tuesday, we fly to Athens

May 4—11/12? October 1967 UK

[We flew from Israel to Athens, and had 2 days there, a day in the city and a day on the beach on the island of Aegina. The army had just seized power in Greece, but our visit was unaffected. We then flew to Geneva and had a few days with our Best Man, Paddy Orr. and his

wife in their lovely chalet in the mountains, where it snowed, an exciting experience for all of us, Aidan in particular.

We flew to U.K. on 4th May.

There are no letters for the period of our leave in the United Kingdom. We made our home with Juliet's parents at Stockton and my mother at Darlington. It was a very difficult time for Juliet, in her mother-in-law's home for much of the time, a relationship only restored when Juliet became hostess in Delhi two years later. I taught at his old school for the first two and a half months The acquisition of a second-hand Ford Prefect car for £30 helped, and enabled us to move between the two homes with Aidan comparatively easily, and also gave us opportunities to travel in the North East, to see friends and other members of our families. In the second half of our leave, we were able to get about into the countryside and in particular to explore Northumberland.

Aidan formed a particularly affectionate relationship with Juliet's father, and ever after back in India talked of Grandpa, his interest in the stars and his 'magic' as a conjuror.

In view of my need to work and earn enough to supplement the college salary, which did not go far in Britain, we declined to take part in the programme of talks and preachments usually expected of missionaries on leave, though I made one brief foray to Cambridge and London to meet with representatives of the mission agencies.

In late June, provision of a sister or brother for Aidan was initiated.

As autumn came on, with shorter and colder days, we rushed around to say our farewells, our minds already on a speedy, unbroken flight back to our home in Delhi in mid-October. We arrived back to the house with a major technical improvement, access to a supply of gas cylinders, for which we had brought back a small gas cooker.

We wrote to the family on the 'homeward' flight and on arrival in Delhi]

BOAC VC10

Dear Mama & Papa

We have just finished our dinner and will soon be in Teheran. It is dark, and I think I have seen Venus!

It was lovely to hear you on the phone, Papa, & to have Mama with us at the airport. We both feel very much for you and Nana at 37, & can only say 'God be with you'.

It has been a good break, but it wd have been nice to have a few more days playing with Aidan in the park. Those autumnal scenes will keep me cool when I remember them in the hot weather. I shall never forget the lovely tints, & the leaves sifting through the trees.

I must say, Mama, I felt very proud of your get-up at the airport. You looked terrific—not bad for 32! Keep it up, old girl!

Aidan was very upset when we left, and wanted to get off the plane! Poor little thing, he really felt the parting. He was sick 40 minutes ago, but then went to sleep at his usual bedtime. He has had a good session of drawing & cutting out and stories, and has planned his sleep very well. We shall probably have a doze after Teheran in preparation for Delhi at dawn.

DELHI. We have just finished lunch in our own house. The Sircars sent breakfast and lunch across to us.

Delhi, November 2, 1967

[This conflates Juliet's letter of this day to her parents with one to her father alone because her mother was away for a few days]

Dear Mama & Papa,

How v v kind of you both to send greeting letters for our return to Delhi. They were much appreciated, and Aidan was thrilled to have his own letter.

Mr. Sircar met us, which was wonderful of him, and we sailed through customs when the officer was told we were going to St. Stephen's. Mr. Sircar took us to their home for a cuppa, & then we went to our house. It had been painted & whitewashed and a new sink put in the kitchen. The curtains had been washed, the furniture polished & we are falling over on the highly shiny floors! All my shopping list had been bought. In fact, a wonderful homecoming!

When we had tea at 5 p.m., we imagined you just beginning to get lunch ready, and the fire on in the dining room

I am having a school session with Aidan every day with the Ladybird Books we brought back with us ... we are putting in the vegetable and flower seeds, and I have just made new net curtains throughout the house. I have also started winter socks for A, and things for No. 2. It is marvellous to have gas in the kitchen, and my little bits of gadgetry make it a safer place. The whole house is so spick & span. Hanson takes a great pride in everything

D is v much submerged in college work and preparation for the Staff Quiet Day.

We are having Dr. Roseveare to dinner tomorrow, and Evelyn again on Wednesday.

The other day, we went to Cottage Industries and bought some lovely brass casserole dishes—all our pyrex is broken, and as the brass is both beautiful and durable, we invested.

All rations have been cut to help meet needs of the famine, so we do not yet know what we shall be allowed.

The garden is parched and needs lots doing to it. We are in the process of putting in seeds for vegetables and flowers. We have a vine growing, so I will send you a bottle of wine.

Aidan said the other night, "I am going to fly into that big tree with Grandpa and catch a star with my fishing net and put it in a jar." He is always saying that Daddy is going to write a letter to tell all the people to come here, and he thinks about you a great deal. Your memory is evergreen!

I know you will know exactly what I mean when I say it is <u>marvellous</u> to be back. I can hardly think of anything more wonderful than being here. I feel that I can say that to you because you will understand that it does not exclude the happy times we had at 37.

Delhi, Nov. 17, 1967

At the vegetable man's stall, I spotted a little scrap of fur, an abandoned kitten, about a week old. As we were wanting a cat, I brought it home. We are feeding it with a medicinal dropper. At first, we had to set the alarm clock and feed it in the middle of the night, but now it sleeps right through. It has gained 2oz. in two weeks. It can't walk very well, but even so follows me about the bedroom, has learnt to purr, & is thriving! Aidan has given it some toys to play with.

We celebrated that pretty Indian festival of lights, Diwali. Aidan was thrilled when I put oil lamps on the window sills, and candles along the path, and we had fireworks. Evelyn was with us and it was a very jolly time.

Looking at the moon the other night, Aidan said 'It's Granpa's moon.'

Across the drive from us is a little settlement of workers who are building the college gymnasium—as I write, in bed, I can hear them singing, and drums.

I have clocked in at St. Stephen's hospital, with Dr. Kavan, whom I very much like, as my doctor, and booked a room for March. If you could please go to the Mothercare shop for me …

Delhi, Nov 29, 1967

I have started making my own bread—lovely brown bread from atta, a great success but not much of an economy as we all eat much more of it, with homemade butter & marmalade.

It is cooling down here, but we are through our change-of-season coughs and colds.

We have had several bachelor invasions after dinner, and were to have had a party but had to cancel when I had Rs. 200 stolen from my bag by a strange workman in the house.

A was thrilled to have a special letter from you, Papa, & has 'read' it several times. He continues to thrive and to add to his vocabulary—latest example, "My knife is too difficult to manage" &, sorting out his supper tray, "Please organise me before I have an accident." His memory & mind seem to develop too—he asked, 'Is Jesus a lady as well as a man? … What do the trees do?' Tell Auntie Sylvia he suddenly remembered the little boy with a kitten at Thornborough. At present, he enjoys drawing, poetry and baking.

D is madly busy—3 new lectures per week, and at least 1 sermon.

Roger Hooker came for a few days, and brought his in-laws, Max & Mrs. Warren to lunch on their way to Agra.

Our veg is thriving, including lots of potatoes … cabbage, cauliflower, brussels sprouts, spinach, tomatoes, onions, leeks, lettuce, turnips & carrots. I have had to pay the equivalent of 2/6 for a lb of sugar—our ration wouldn't keep us in tea sugar for a month (and I don't take any, D hardly any).

Thurs - today, we shall go to buy some baking tins.

Delhi, Dec. 7, 1967

D has just posted a letter to Hilda & Bill to thank them for the glorious Selfridge's food parcel—it has 'made' our Christmas!

This letter will be a day late because we daren't post it locally for fear of the mobs setting a light to the box—we are having lots of student / political unrest. The college has been closed for 2 days—nothing to be worried about, but rather inconvenient.

Last Friday, Evelyn came and did the honours so that we could go to the college performance of 'Richard III'. (She wears that brooch you gave her constantly). On Sunday, we went to the St James Garden Fete, and it was nice to see everyone again.

The taxi fares have gone up, so we are more marooned than before—though we did manage to go to New Delhi, and bumped into our nurse, Mary Earnshaw.

A is now learning C Carols.

The ration of sugar is 4½ lbs per month, and is Rs.1.20 per kilo, but we can get more in the bazaar at Rs.5. The UK devaluation means our Child Allowance is down Rs.15

Delhi, Dec. 16, 1967

Very many thanks for the parcel, Mama—please tell me how much I owe you [she very rarely did tell us].

Very wintry weather here, cold & grey.

Student riots… the University has had to be closed for a few days, and we had to have a pass to enter or leave the area. The Reserve Police (tin hats, big sticks) were on duty at our corner & everyone was carefully checked. Mobs forced us to close the college day after day, until the crackpot vice-chancellor had to be told to close down the University … it is rather pleasant to be on holiday already.

I've put the almond paste on the Christmas cake, & A & I are going to make Christmas decorations soon. Catlet can now lap from a saucer. Veg is growing, and the bulbs we brought back with us.

We're having Leonard Schiff, the Westcott-Teape Lecturer to dinner on Thursday.

There is never a dull moment with A—he can point out 8 different birds correctly, & can plant cabbage seedlings properly. He put himself to bed in the afternoon, and said v proudly that he didn't bother Mummy when she was resting. He loves sewing, and threading buttons and can remember the process of plain knitting. He likes to have a mid-morning snack in a paper bag. When he wakes up in the morning at 6.30 a.m., he sits at his nursery table looking at books or drawing until the tea comes … he adores looking at those big art books that you gave me. We took him to see the police patrol at the corner, and he says that he's going to be a policeman one day and 'bash all the cars'. His favourite supper is egg & chips.

This must be a letter of greeting for the 25th … we shall drink a toast to you in lime juice—you will have to compensate with s'thing a little stronger. A & I hope to get to D's 6.30 a.m. Communion at the hospital.

* * * * *

1968 PARENTS AGAIN

Delhi, Jan. 5, 1968

On Christmas Day, I cooked—Hanson is beginning to prove unreliable.

D took the midnight at St. James & then we all went to the hospital service at 6.30 a.m., wh D took, he then went back to assist at St. James at 8, and on to St. Stephen's in Fatehpuri bazaar, home for lunch. Evelyn for lunch. An old friend came and talked in the kitchen while I baked for 16 college boys who came to tea. It all went down v well!

The main item in A's stocking was a hammer and a big selection of nails! I made a chest of matchboxes covered in coloured paper, and each drawer had a different type of nail. He also got a funnel, tin kettle and a milk-measure just like the dudewallah's. These & sweets have kept him happy ever since. He has also found a piece of rope, and claims he has a dog on the other end, which keeps getting into rabbit holes. Where does he get these ideas?!

26th - Roger came from Agra to stay for a few days,
27th - Aryas for tea plus old friend, and a new friend for dinner.
28th - 2 young medics for dinner.
29th - Roger left, friend for tea.
30th - Pat arrived from Agra.
1st - Pat moved out for one night, and new artist friend, Jyoti Sahi, stayed.

2nd - Pat returned, left 6.30 a.m. on 3rd. We took Aidan to a Junior Jet Club (BOAC) party at the Gymkhana Club in N Delhi.

Today, Evelyn has been for the evening.

Unfortunately, Hanson was off for two days, just when I was beginning to feel worn out *[6 months pregnant]* He was late this morning, and Aidan opened the door to him and said, 'Have you been on your holidays?'

Asked what he wanted for tea one day, A reeled off a long list, including sausages, so I asked what he thought he'd get, and he said 'peanuts'. Pat asked him what he'd had for supper one night, and he said, "Not chips". He keeps us laughing.

How kind of you to knit me a sweater. I've been trying to wangle the housekeeping to buy some wool for sweaters for Aidan, and have come to the conclusion I shall have to wait until another year!

We have decided not to leave Delhi this summer, too much for a 2-month old baby, and will hire some sort of air cooler … we feel v happy with this decision, We shall raid the library at the beginning of the holiday, and settle down for a homely time together. I've now read 12 Trollopes— reading makes me knit quickly.

Monday—the wretch *[Hanson]* is off again—3 days, so I am v busy

Delhi, Jan. 13, 1968. Sunday morn

A gloriously sunny morning, and I am sitting out under the nursery window. Aidan is playing with 'Catty', and is full of cold and has croup. I've got some dope for him, but slept in his room last night.

I have a 'snorter' too. We have school every day, and that is great fun—y'day, we made a nature table like the one in his Ladybird book.

D continues to be as busy as ever, and in fact is doing some extra work—he has been asked to write a book on T.S.Eliot's 'Four Quartets'—it will help with the general purse.

On the 9th, we had a lovely birthday tea for A+D—I made a cake with 3 candles—and jelly and ice cream. Evelyn came. A had a present and card from Sircars. A student called Nirupam Sen gave him 'Alice in Wonderland' *[Nirupam Sen, later, India's Ambassador to the United Nations]*. A was remembering playing in the coalhouse at 37 & going fishing with Granpa.

We had a trip to ND, and bought some nappies.
On Friday, we had, at their request, a bachelor party
We are now eating cabbage and lettuce, and spinach soup, from the garden.
Today, we have 2 girls fm Darlington to stay overnight, and their adventures make me feel positively ancient.
Must go & put the bread in the oven—we are again cook-less today.

Delhi, Feb. 7, 1968

The pram has been re-covered in preparation for No.2,, & I have nearly finished my sewing. We have had the verandah trellis extended so we have a really secure extra room for summer.

I do much of my grocery shopping at Mr Sood's 'Iceland' in KamlaNagar. He is v obliging.

Thank you for sending yet another 'baby parcel'.

For goodness sake stop flapping about March—we shall manage perfectly well. Danny is to take some leave, and is perfectly well able to look after Aidan completely

A's latest—'that blinking cat is a nuisance'.

He says that when I go to hospital, he will take my bag and purse and do the shopping, and come and feed me sultanas in bed!

He loves to sew, and has made several toys with rattling buttons for the cat, and intends to make some for the baby.

He gave D a lecture about the dentist at 5.30 a.m.

Delhi, Feb. 13, 1968

… waiting for "Number Two". Delhi is warm now, & we need only sheets on the bed and perhaps a blanket at dawn.

The postman has just brought the most gorgeous parcel. How can we thank you enough. We are having prunes tonight. The cardboard from the parcel will go round the celery. A has got the box to play with (the last box is used by the cat to sleep in).

The Feb 'Housewife' has arrived already, plus Echo and Gazette.

I am embroidering a kneeler for the chapel in Durham Castle, D's old college.

D had to go to N Delhi today, and thought I looked glum, so brought back some pork chops—what a treat! He puts A to bed these days, and very well he manages it, too.

Delhi, Feb. 18, 1968

Y'day, I deserted the boys and went to a sale of work at the Rajpur Rd community and stocked up w tray-cloths for another year!.

Our neighbour's hens have been eating our veg, so the other day, I caught the fattest of them, and shut it in the kitchen until they repaired the wire-netting fence—result, proper fencing, and the college got a laugh, and our neighbour gave me a goose egg, so no hard feelings! She and Mrs. Sircar have both given me goose eggs in the past, and I make a special cake with them.

It seems at last to be warming up a bit 47-73—D & I are sitting on the verandah, both wearing sweaters—just for a bit of tropical atmosphere, I've just heard a peacock.

Only an hour before the postman arrived, we had arranged a loan from college, but now we can cancel that and not be in debt—you naughty, kind, generous things! The money will cover the cost of having the pram covered, some of the air-cooler rent, and help buy some sludge for the veg garden. I was completely stunned when the postman arrived.

What news of Hilda & Bill? We are so looking forward to their visir after the baby has arrived.

Delhi, Mar. 3, 1968

Yes, again sitting on the verandah in the glorious sunshine , the purple sunbirds hovering by the tree.

Mrs. Sircar often calls, swaps magazines and veg

We've just heard—Hilda & Bill will arrive on the 29th, Hilda to stay for a few days, while Bill goes to the south on business! Isn't it exciting?!

[constantly, Juliet acknowledges letters from her father to Aidan, plus photos sent by D's sister Kath of A's cousin Matthew, similar age]

Delhi, March 21, 1968

Well—another grandson for you: Timothy Patrick— born 5.35 a.m. 7lbs 4 oz (1lb lighter than A). He kept us waiting for 11 days, & in fact last night I was admitted to hosp in preparation for the doctor to induce labour today. Mrs. Sircar baby sat with A last night, and the Principal brought D & me in his car. At 2.30 a.m., I woke up, and this fellow was obviously on his way. Two hours later, I walked to the labour room & sat around for ½ hour. He was born 3 hrs from start to finish—everyone was surprised—I still can't believe it! At lunch time today, I walked around the room & am feeling very fit & happy.

D is very thrilled—naturally—& A also. He took one look at me, and said, 'Where's our little baby?' Mummy is very dull now!

Timothy has a lot of hair, brownish blond and blue eyes and is a carbon copy of A and D! He has a loud voice, & is v active. As I write this, it is 7.15 p.m., so he is 13 hours old, and sleeping peacefully in a crib at my side.

I had insisted on a walk right along the Ridge y'day afternoon … perhaps that hurried him up.

[24 March—letter from J in hospital to D's mother—we are going to have Holy Communion in my room this morning.]

Juliet and Aidan at Timothy's Christening

Delhi, March 30, 1968

I'm in the sitting-room with your ambassadors *[Hilda &
Bill Bamforth]*

Thank you for the goodies –fabulous—also Rs.100—I
intend buying some more blanket wool and a second plastic
bucket!

We had a home day, with a walk round college, and H &
B did a stint in the garden this afternoon.

I continue to be very fit, & so is Timothy—also A, who
helps me bath T, & D is still seeing to A's routine.

A is trying to teach T to talk.
Mon. Bill went off to Bombay this morning, and today
Hilda has really earned her keep as baby-rocker in chief.
We hope to get one or two trips into ND.

The cooler was installed this morning, (mostly paid for
with money from H & B) and seems to be v efficient, so we
are all set to face the summer.

Delhi, April 15, 1968

We did enjoy Hilda & Bill's visit, but they seemed to be
whisked away so quickly that it is hard to believe they have
been. H made herself v useful, ironing & pram pushing,
amusing Aidan & being a general dogsbody. Please tell
them how much I appreciated it.

We have now settled into a routine, and T has slept right through the last 3 or 4 nights.

I had my hospital check-up today, and all is well, and T was weighed—9/6—I cd hardly believe he had gained so much.

He is already cooing, and loves to talk to the nursery curtain, as A did. A is always kissing him and saying what a nice little boy he is. He has also given T his panda, and loves to help with the bath and pram-pushing. I have just got him some cool Indian clothes for the baptism.

"Mummy, are ears for telephoning ... when Catty dies, I'm going to live in his box".

No doubt Papa will not believe it, but I shall be 26 this year, and that + 2 children makes me feel v ancient & responsible!

With the help at various stages of A and D, I made 13½ lbs of marmalade the other day ... jam & chutney to follow very soon. Please air-mail me some jam-pot covers.

Melons & mangoes are in season, so we have them brought to the door.

Delhi, April 29, 1968

Timothy has been ill, so you can imagine how full the days—and nights—have been. He is now fully recovered, but seems to have a rather delicate tummy, so we have to be extra careful, but he can coo and gurgle a bit now.

The baptism went off very pleasantly. Dr. Rosevears stood proxy for Juliet's former school friend, Carol Bonsall, and T & A both behaved perfectly. D's friend Michael Keeling was godfather.

We had seven boys to an end-of-term tea the other day, & Evelyn babysat on Friday to enable us to go to the staff dinner. Tonight, we are having an end-of-term bachelor party, outside in the cool (it was 102 today).

A is giving a running commentary on his 'office work' as I try to write this. He appeared in the kitchen during his 'rest' the other day with a great dripping basket of clothes. He was very proud because he had taken everything out of the linen bag and done the washing for me!! We hung it on the line, a rather motley cleanliness.

Hope you will be able to have Mrs. Sircar *[going to UK for a month on a Mother's Union programme—she also visited Juliet's aunt and uncle in a Yorkshire village, Thornborough, and D's mother]*

Delhi, May 15, 1989

We are all flourishing. T now weighs a little over 13 lbs—not bad going for 7 weeks! He is very 'talkative' and a great joy, but I have no one to show him off to!

Mary Earnshaw baby-sat so we could go out for dinner … The dinner was ruined by an unexpected addition to the party. *[Gilpatric, CIA?]* He is responsible for distributing Rockefeller millions in Asia, but is a horrid flirty old man (not nice flirty).

Nirupam Sen. one of D's students he is v fond of, a v brilliant boy, arrived w presents for all of us! He gave me a gorgeous silk evening bag!

[We survived a summer vacation at home, thanks to the cooler in one room, but the children were troubled with heat-exhaustion. Evelyn Reading finished work in India in June; she was very eccentric, but was greatly missed by all of us, Juliet in particular]

Delhi, June 3, 1968

A said the other day he was a Back-Door-Mouse, also was playing at being the dhobi, but said that he was "<u>not</u> the blinking dhobi who washes all the buttons off". He adores T and T adores him.

Every night, ox carts go past the gate laden with melons, and the pavements in Kamla Nagar are piled high with them.

We have had frightful dust storms. One lasted 36 hours. Minimum temp 91, goes up to 106 at present.

The milkmen have gone on strike for the right to sell adulterated milk.

Delhi, June 24, 1968

We are absolutely thrilled by your unexpected plan of a holiday in Edinburgh. Do please write a full account.

I have given the cook a holiday—there is no fan in the kitchen, so you can imagine what I look like by lunchtime. The monsoon is forecast for 29th June. We don't go anywhere in this heat, but we are all very well.

Another attempted burglary next door at Aryas'—the second in about 3 weeks. We heard the commotion. They got away in a taxi. When will it be our turn?

Delhi, July 5, 1968

Food prices up, including eggs that a pigeon would be ashamed of.

Mrs. Sircar is v excited—most, she wants to see the English countryside and villages. Your plans for her sound wonderful

TP is up to my baby-book weight, and is such a cheerful baby … just itching to be running round with A. We are thrilled with him, and don't want him to grow up too quickly!

I have not been out since TP was 2 weeks old, except to Kamla Nagar for an hour each month, and dinner at Maiden's Hotel one evening, but this afternoon Mary Earnshaw is going to babysit, and D & I are going to ND. It will be wonderful to have a break. We did, all 4, get to the 6.15 a.m. Communion in the Brotherhood garden on Ascension Day.

Delhi, July 27, 1968

The monsoon started with several glorious sunsets, and then we awoke on the verandah with v wet feet, and retreated to dry sheets indoors. Aidan's word for a blanket is wintersheet. He has just recovered from a cold and TP is nearly better—he was really very poorly. I got some dope fm the hospital & he is much improved—I seemed to do nothing but nurse him day & night for some time. He never takes his eyes off A and A's doings.

D took A to the zoo about 2 weeks ago. I gave them a picnic & off they went in a rickshaw. Its been zoo ever since. "I would like a monkey, Mummy. I can carry it in my little arms and you can carry the cage".

I made apricot and plum jam in their absence—far too popular to be economical!
A's crochet blanket will soon be finished. I've taught myself quite a bit from my little French needlework book, and intend doing some finer work with the cotton Hilda gave me.

What a marvellous time you had in Edinburgh, espy books and art.

Tues. Y'day, we were having a couple of friends in for a drink (their booze!)—I slipped with a pyrex dish in my hand, & nearly cut off my index finger ... rushed to hosp by a neighbour while D had A & T ... four stitches and a smashing bandage, and D is doing the nappies.

We've had to chase a monkey away from the garden recently. Also, a cheeky cat came into our bedroom while we were all asleep after T's 6 o'clock feed, and stole his bottle wh had a bit of milk left in it. I woke up to clinking noises and gave chase in my nightie and retrieved the bottle as the cat jumped through the hedge!

Since term resumed, I've managed to get both of them to chapel each Sunday ... both boys are v good there.

Delhi, August 10, 1968

Thank you also for A's letter—he keeps re-'reading' it ... Thank you for looking after Mrs. Sircar so well. We had a letter from her & she was absolutely thrilled at all you did for her. Do thank Auntie Sylvia & Uncle John too—you all rallied so well. We had Mr. Sircar in for dinner the other night.

Well, the really great news is that we have sold our soul to the Provident Fund & bought a WASHING MACHINE, ... locally made, called Everest ... The dhobi has gradually got things greyer and greyer, and for the last few months I have had to wash practically everything by hand. I can't believe how clean everything is—cost Rs.534, and worth every paise!

The hot weather vegs we planted are as tall as I am, and if we get as many pumpkins as there are flowers, we shall have a whole fleet of golden coaches.

We've had ten days of gorgeous sun and now are back in pouring rain.

T is such a firm sitter-up, and full of smiles. A is kite mad, and goes through lots. He and D went to the river Jumna the other day on the scooter (A stands on the footboard), and I must say they saw everything—boats, monkeys, tractors.

Sunday chapel again tomorrow—A is allowed to snuff out the candles. It is odd how vivid Sunday mornings at 37 are, a real landmark in my memory.

I occasionally give A an 'old numbers' concert, and he thinks it great—wd be grateful for full words of Burlington Bertie, please.

Delhi, August 25, 1968

It gives me great pleasure to know that Sylvia *[Sylvia Riley, college friend]* has been with you.

We have had a run of crises—my finger, D's got kidney stones—he's taking dope to get rid of them He also has a bad knee. T teething, and needs constant cuddles. Fortunately I brought Woodward's teething drops back with us. His teething (and weight) are further on than A's at this age. A has an awful blistering skin infection, and is having penicillin injections, and TP has just begun it too.

I am v fit—just as well, as Hanson has been off a week—but, bless his heart, Babu Lal turned up & took over, saying I was v busy because I had 2 babies.

Apart from above troubles, T is bursting with health and happiness. He splashes in the bath like mad. His hair is growing quickly—nearly white. He is more of an introvert than Aidan—that is the impression we get.

"How many brothers have you, Aidan?" "Two, Timmy and me". A spends a great deal of time writing "essays" in his "tutorial book". He asked to have a working breakfast in his nursery because he said he was so busy.

Mary Earnshaw babysat TP for us on our anniversary on the 17th and we took A to ND and had pink ice cream. Mary cdnt resist giving T a bath! Not that he needed one.

We have had a few holidays because mobs forced us to close the college. Quite lively, I must say. We hear them shouting, but not near us.

I have started knitting for the winter. The crochet blanket is nearly finished & looks v pretty.

D has now finished his bk on T S Eliot, and we are going shopping to spend the money he's got for paper and typing.

Catty is as lovable and daft as ever, and refuses all milk except Lactogen—he is a Snob.

As I write, the crickets are chirping like mad and the fan is whizzing round, and there is a lizard on the wall.

Delhi, Sept 4, 1968

A is thrilled with the shirts you sent. I said to him that they were a bit big. "No, Mummy, nice & cool".

2 Cambridge chaplains and the brother of one of them turned up—they have left the brother, Stephen Courtauld with us, very pleasant but a bit mixed up—we are providing a bolthole for him—he took us out to dinner at the Ashoka … a fabulous evening, 'lashed up to the nines', smashing food and booze, cabaret and old-time music. Lifted me right out of teething troubles and I felt like a million dollars—with compliments to match!. We've had a week of good talk, always into the next day. A & Stephen get on v

well together. I think we have helped him. He had a break-down about a year ago. Poor boy (2 years older than I) has so much money, he doesn't quite know what to do. He wants his life to be useful and his money used for good ... sensitive & compassionate ... he is going to our friends at Naini Tal, and will be back later

Delhi, Oct. 1, 1968

Delhi troubles ... strikes ... mobs ... armed police ... baton charges ... tear gas ... I've not dared to go out to post a letter until now. A letter from UK took 13 days.

I am knitting Fair Isle sweaters for the 2 boys, & reading Mrs. Gaskell "Sylvia's Lovers".

We have 2 weeks holiday, so D is putting A to bed—TP having long gone (he slept 13 hours last night. He is full of smiles. Lots of lovely fair hair.

Mr. Sircar is ill—blood pressure. D has been to see him in the hospital.

We have just got the veg plots going, & D is going for seeds & seedlings on Thurs.

At A's request, I re-told A the Marriage at Cana miracle the other day, and, when he was having his supper, he put milk and butter into a glass of water and explained that he had changed it into wine. His drawing is getting better & better. I have been to see 2 nursery schools, and hope to start him at the better of them—everything depends on whether USPG will pay the fees *[they did]*.

TP has three teeth, and the 4th will surely arrive within the next 24 hours

9 Oct. sorry for the delay, but I am in the middle of flu' and dysentery.

Recvd y'day the 'Ideal Home' mag you posted on 1st July. We look fwd to yr kind parcels … fantastically generous.

What time of year would you think of coming, Mama ?

Delhi, Nov. 20, 1968

Thanks for lovely postcards for A. He has a scrap book for such things.

Stephen Courtauld came back for 10 days … the Ashoka again, the nightclub … fantastic food. Eventually, after a few false starts, he has gone off to Kashmir.

Since then … such a run of illness that I am run off my feet and worried out of my wit s. D—kidney stones … x-rays etc … then I was unwell with my back, but only for 24 hours … A had pains in his knees and is being treated for vitamin C deficiency … and this past week, TP has been very very poorly with tummy and vomiting—unfortunately, D had to go to Agra to do a Quiet Day, & I had the worst day with T and had to go back to hospital with him. I slept beside him in the nursery for 4 nights. I'm now full of cold and tired, not surprisingly.

On the bright side, A has started school—like a duck to water!—Playways on Mall Road, 5 mins by taxi (but D will usually take him by scooter)… a v good school in every respect—they do marvellous things—glowing reports of his conversation, writing etc and how well he behaves and makes friends. He went to a party in Cavalry Lines, y'day, fab house, roundabouts, performing monkeys and bears, films, a train—the little boy was only 4—what will they do when he's 21! A came home with paper fez askew—what a sight!

Some students took him to the college café for coca cola, & I have glowing reports of that, too.

Hanson has left, & I now have a lady cook—Sabra, a Muslim widow of the principal's bearer, Hanif, with 5 children. She is learning everything from scratch, and shaping well. She was one of my knitting ladies, so we are good friends. I went to visit her when Hanif died, and have done what I can for the family. With her 6 words of English and my half dozen of Hindustani, we manage famously!

Babu Lal's son, Maurice, has just got married. We went to the wedding.

At present we have a lovely planet, liquid silver, low in the S.W at evening—what is it, Daddy?

There is a nip in the air 83-55—have just taken out winter clothes.

Delhi, Dec. 3, 1968

A wonderful Christmas hamper from Hilda & Bill, and another from you! Our C/Cake is assured, and a deal of good fare besides. We really cannot thank you enough for all your kindness. I am also constantly reminded of you by the gorgeous blue cardigan you sent. I truly do not know how I would keep warm without it.

We are now, thank Heaven, all well. Immediately after TP's frightening gastric 'do', he had a heavy cold. He is at the Lactogen Book weight for 1 year, and I am having to knit him bigger things. Both boys have lovely rosy cheeks now the colder weather is here—they have great frolics on the bed. T is trying to talk.... Such good reports of A at school—I feel a terribly proud Mum. I said to him y'day. "Are there any kind fairies to go and bring Mummy's work-basket"—"No, they are all on holiday".

And ...

A "Who is that?"

M "A new college lecturer"

A "What happened to the old one?"

And -

He asked what happens at the station when the train stops.

M "The people get out and new people get in"

A "And do they have smooth skin & new faces?!

He has a girl friend in school, who bosses him about, and calls herself "Mrs. Aidan".

My new Muslim cook, Sabra is getting on v well—I have to cook the bacon, and keep it well wrapped, but otherwise she does anything. Since Babu Lal left, we have turned his room into a guest room.

Mary Earnshaw babysat, so we cd get to the college production of "Love's Labour's Lost"

Stephen is back from Kashmir, in bed with 'flu for a week—he brought us a lovely rug for the sitting room, a beautiful carved box for D and a lovely painted one for me, and a model houseboat for A. and a silk waistcoat, so we are waiting for the next party invitation. Can you imagine, S pays 19/9 in the £ income tax and can still swan around the world, money no object!

My hair is quite long now, and much admired, so I shall keep it so, at least until the next hot weather.

We shall have a VSO boy with us for Christmas, son of the Rector of Stepney ... we felt we cd not refuse a Christmas stranger.

Delhi, Dec. 13, 1968

Thank you for identifying Venus, Daddy—gorgeous again tonight.

A has had a cold and looks a bit thin, but I have found him Kepler's malt & shark liver oil, and we are cramming in vits. And Marmite. His school report is all Excellents— I'm bursting with motherly pride! He says Sheila's Mummy has "an older face than you, all nice and wrinkly"., The mothers are a new world of contacts for me. When he wdnt settle for his rest one afternoon:
A. "I'm like the clock, Mummy"
M "What do you mean"
A. "Moving round"
We will go shopping in ND to fill two Christmas stockings this year.

We are eating turnips, spinach & lettuce from the garden. A has his own veg garden this year, and knows exactly how to plant and water things. He is also in charge of the compost, and makes sure nothing is thrown away.

Delhi, Dec. 28, 1968

The VSO turned up, a nice boy, going to work for White Horse whisky on Islay, so we've booked our fishing holiday! He was a delightful guest, and we had a lovely C Day. Stephen C, who we thought had gone to Africa, also turned up loaded with presents.

Christmas Eve, tea at Sircar's, and the Bishop's wife asked Mr. Sircar who that young girl was—made my day!

D took A to St James children's service—carols round the crib—A's photo was in the paper twice, once in the crowd, once on his own lighting a candle. Of course we are delighted, but what a pity they didn't choose an Indian child. On Christmas morning, D & I and the boys went to the 6.30 at the hospital, and D took the service—nice because we have so many friends there. Just for once, we had to miss out the students' Christmas Day tea.

A had plasticine in his stocking, so he's made a plasticine switch and fixed it to a candle so you can switch it on.

D & I bought each other a tea trolley.

Sabra's oldest son presented me with a beautiful silver filigree brooch, & Mary Earnshaw a silk scarf—what luxuries! Our Cambodian Buddhist monk friend came with cards and sweets, and Mrs. Sircar a lovely lace dinner set— we have been showered with lovely things—so v v kind

Chicken for lunch w all the trimmings, followed by Indian halva, carrot pudding.

Our electric fire broke finally on Boxing Day—Stephen disappeared, and came back with two! Our friend Balbir Singh came for supper.

Poor little Tim is not well—he has had croup, cold and cough for a month, and I have slept in the nursery, trying different medicines w Dr. Roseveare's help—we have cancelled our evening entertaining for the present, though the Aryas will come to tea on Thursday.

D will post this at Kash Gate on his way to see Nirad Chaudhuri, the writer.

* * * * *

1969 GRANDMOTHERLY VISITORS

Delhi, Jan. 4, 1969

From Christmas on, Tim has been v v poorly—Dr. Roseveare visited twice on Monday, the second time, at night, deciding he must go straight into hospital, so we went to Kalavati Saran Children's Hospital in New Delhi, where he had oxygen immediately and 5 different injections. , D took slides for analysis to another hospital. For 48 hours, they thought it might be diphtheria, but it was acute spasmodic bronchitis. They do not have private rooms, but we got one to ourselves, at least at first (rather dirty) and again after D caused a great fuss, and a kind doctor whom we knew arranged for my meals to be sent or (with hot baths) at her house, when her daughter babysat. I was so depressed and worried at one point that D secretly asked Jennifer Thorpe from St Stephen's Community to come and stay over one night. The Children's Hospital gave me the horrors, but on Thursday, we were transferred to St Stephen's Hospital, which felt like coming home, given a guest room in the doctors' residence, where Mary Earnshaw has cuddled T and coddled me! I had hardly slept for some weeks, and now feel rested and much better. It is now Saturday evening, and we are going home tomorrow. D & A have managed, and been able to visit together. A has twice been looked after by the Arya's, and once by Sheila's mother.

Now I am all set to face the new year, and get this little baby absolutely better.

Delhi, Jan. 27, 1969

Am sitting on the verandah, v sunny but a slightly chill breeze. Tim is gurgling, and trying to crawl on a rug at my feet. He is still waking a lot with coughing during the night, but otherwise very alright.

A had an accident the other day, got scalded, not badly but has a few nasty blisters on foot, leg, hand and arm. His <u>immediate</u> reaction was to ask to go to Chapel to say his prayers. We had some at home, and D had to say more when he came in, and even then it was difficult to explain why he could not go and lie in Chapel on his bed. He had that day off school, rather shocked, but now is fully re-covered.

Where are you going for your hol, Mama? Why not come to Delhi ?!! Don't faint, this is a definite invitation. The cook's room is now available as a guest room. Now do make an effort for heaven's sake, and don't cry about it. There are loads of cheap charter flights to fly out relatives of missionaries at cheap rates. D's mother has the details. Get cracking!

Delhi, March 2, 1969

We decided not to go to the Republic Day parade this year, but D took A on the scooter to see the Beating of the Retreat. The school went to the zoo the next day—a won-derful time.

Y'day we went to an Arya sister's wedding … lovely din-ner. Sabra looked after A &T—a real boon she is.

Last Sunday we went to a Brotherhood tea party—very nice to see everyone. I get so few opportunities.

TP is now v healthy, but I was still up a lot at night with his coughing until recently, and got v tired. A is thriving & loving school. D is working at the same old pace.

I now have a v nice young American friend, Norleen Shelton, with a boy and girl a bit younger than A & T. I introduced her to A's school, and her boy now goes there. She picks us up & takes us to school. We get on SO well—she is in a similar position to me friendwise. We have now got to the point of swapping clothes, & she has just given me a great bag of clothes for TP which her boy has outgrown. They are Methodist missionaries.

After this, I'm going to write my groceries list for Mr. Sood. Have taken my friend & shown her Kamla Nagar—she is thrilled to find such a good bazaar so near.

[Norleen Shelton, as the only other young non-Indian mother in our part of Old Delhi during these years, became a good friend to Juliet for the rest of our time in India—and beyond. She wrote subsequently, "Besides being beautiful, she was gentle and always a lady. She was wise, calm, kind, thoughtful, creative, resourceful, and never complained. I remember her wry sense of humour, and her shy smile , with her eyes twinkling. She accepted people as they were. Actually, I have never found another friend with her unique qualities]

Delhi, March 14, 1969

TP is now 26 lbs! now v vocal, & can shout with the best of them. He loves playing with Sabra, so I can leave him whilst I go to the bazaar—a big relief.

How kind of you to send a toys parcel.

Last Saturday, I had an afternoon off at Mary Earn-shaw's—she put me to bed with a good novel & oranges. Then tea in bed, and a lovely bottle of scent as a present.

We have got very friendly with the Japanese exchange student, & had a delightful evening of paper folding (origami).

D has been v unwell with kidney trouble—he was all set to go to Ludhiana hospital for surgery when, miraculously, the stone popped out. No trouble since.

We've decided to stay here this summer, but won't be able to afford a cooler.

Delhi, Easter Day, April 10, 1969

On Good Friday, D baby sat, so I could go to the 3 Hours at St. James. I thought of you, Mama, going to the Yarm church in your lunch break. D went on Saturday evening to Jaipur for Easter services, and is due back on Monday morning.

We've had an artist friend, Jyoti Sahi, staying with us— the first of a line of bachelors who have booked up with us! We had a dinner party for Jyoti with his mother and fiancée Jane.

We all 4 went to tea with 80-years old Dr. Bouquet from Cambridge last week, and had Tony & Ursula King from the Indian Inst of Technology for lunch one day, and went to my American friends one evening—delicious American food.

We've bought a pressure cooker with a repaid compulsory loan to Govt in 1963—great economy on gas.

We've hung chick-screens on the nursery windows in preparation for it getting hotter this summer.

I am having trouble with a knee and hope its not arthritis [first mention]

I'm pulling out old sweaters and crocheting a blanket—I've got the bug, say I'll just do a line, and can't stop! Roshan Lal, who does the theatre costumes to my designs, has been making shirts and trousers for A and shirts for D

D took A to the circus (T too young, we felt)—A, on return, "Mummy, lions, but they didn't eat us". We've had circus performances ever since.

We've had our little guest room whitewashed, and got some pretty curtains. You will like it!

Delhi, April 27, 1969

V sorry for long delay, but I have not been well—Vitamin B deficiency—painful joints, esp leg —also exhaustion—trying to take it gently, but not easy at this time of year, as students are leaving—12 for coffee one night, and 12 for tea y'day, and 4 separate coffees this morning, and a difficult casual guest.

TP & A have bad coughs—a treacherous time of year—but a v good new doctor, Natarajan, so I am not worried.

At the moment, D is marking exam papers—shd pay for a fan for Sabra in the kitchen.

A is loving school. We have got him a place at the British School from January. He is v witty, and bursting with ideas. He has just seen a silent Charlie Chaplin film and pretends to be CC.

TP now has 10 teeth and 2 imminent. Loves to stand, with help, and has a great sense of humour.

I have just made myself some new cotton dresses to replace various decrepit rags—has boosted my morale no end. I always wear lipstick now, and v often eye shadow. I have to look smart to take A to school! We had our annual staff dinner last night, & it was v nice to dress up & meet people—my lady cook is a v good ayah when necessary. We've just entertained a guest for dinner—casual & v nice, but that's the way we go on & on & on.

Delhi, May 14, 1969

Greetings for your two birthdays—32 years old again, Mother?!

How marvellous to be off to Edinburgh—I do envy you the lovely little wandering places, & I'm longing to get into a good 2nd hand bookshop with lots of pocket money.

I am v much better, but my leg is still a bit troublesome and I think it may be a bit arthritic.

D's mother is coming in July, so I must get busy and dust behind the toolshed. We are looking fwd to her visit and to yours later.

We have 14 bunches of grapes on the vine outside the kitchen door, and we've just planted cucumbers, marrows, and melons in the garden.

We have dinner on the verandah these evenings, & it is v pleasant in the scent of jasmine and the tropical night noises—just like a BBC play!

Mary Earnshaw is doing a great tidy out before she goes, and has passed on several v useful items, dress & house.

David Goslin, Physics lecturer and a big help to D at chapel, has just left (we had a farewell dinner the night before), & we inherited much of his property, blankets etc. This seems to happen to us a lot, and we remember our friends all over the house.

Delhi, May 19, 1969

Dear Papa. I'm so pleased to think of you in dear old Edinburgh. We all hope you are having a very interesting & happy holiday. I am longing to get into a good second-hand bookshop with lots of pocket money. We do love to get your separate letters, and A delights in his special bits.

We've just taken a guest, Julian Reindorp, to the station (his father is Bp of Guildford & he went to D's theological college). No more guests now until D's Mum.

D is playing with A & TP—A says Granpa is 'the funny tricks man'—D is carrying out buckets of water so they can go in the paddling pool.

Delhi, June 3, 1969

The students are all away, and lots of the staff.

We are in the grips of the hot weather—the electric supply is v erratic—half the time, the fridge is off, so when we get our milk supply, we have to drink it immediately.

D was giving TP a drink of water, and A asked to do so "Because it will make God happy". We've hired a fan for the kitchen.

A -"Bottoms are only good for falling down on".
Seeing a bird's nest with a bit of cellophane in it, I said wasn't the bird clever to weave the nest —"Ah, but it needed the cellotape to stick it together".

I had a secular Quiet Day at Mary's last week—novel, sewing and ham sandwiches.

Delhi, June 18, 1969

Well, the PARCEL has arrived. *[school-bag for A]* He went to bed with it beside him the first night, then I put it in the cupboard, but he woke D in the middle of the next night and made him put it by his bed to be ready for the morning. The stickers are on the nursery doors, and D & I sat up late in bed with the Andy Capp cartoons and St. Peter's parish magazines. *[letter includes in A's writing 'Thank you for the lovely parcel'].*

TP is v perky, and climbing onto chairs. They are playing together a lot. After a difference with A the other day, I said "We shall see". He went away muttering, "I shall see. You won't see". He is v good at sewing on buttons. Instead of the usual bedtime "O'Reilly" story, he asked D for "a chat about the parcel". D found him painting in the nursery at 5 the other morning.

The Sircars took us to India Gate one evening, and we bumped into the Alvas *[both MPs, she Deputy-Chair of the Rajya Sabha]*

The weather is fluctuating, up to 108 (cool for the time of year!), down to 79. D has prickly heat, but the rest of us seem to have escaped.

I've finished my tapestry for D's college at Durham, and Mary will bring it home.
Now … embroidery and crochet—can you imagine me in these pursuits!

Delhi, July 14, 1969

[D's mother has arrived—Thanks for presents brought by her]

[In preparation for her arrival] … the whitewashers came, and we had 3 days of chaos. I washed, amongst others, the bedroom curtains, and they fell to pieces—wasn't that lucky, —erm, I mean unfortunate—we are now v smart with lacy curtains in a leafy tapestry design.

We met D's mother on the dot at Palam airport—A was rigid w excitement. We were home within an hour. Unfortunately, the next morning, she was unwell with, we think, heatstroke. The monsoon broke last night, but until then it was very hot. If she is still unwell tomorrow, we will call our doctor.

She has a complete 'Granny kit' of sweets & surprises in her cupboard, & A knows it!

A restarted school today, and is v happy, and since he came home has been singing about it. He had very little play with other children during the hot weather. I have found it v difficult to keep both him and TP happy during the long hot summer indoors. TP is quite worn out with the heat, and keeps flopping on the floor, and his appetite is poor ... (I made fudge for us all to eat when we weren't interested in food). I hope the new liquidiser will enable me to produce all sorts of concoctions of the right consistency for him. Perhaps this time next year I shall be wondering why I worried—but I do.

I'm sure when you come you will find me very dull and a bit odd. The other day, Panda Ghose, the bursar's daughter, took me to the University Coffee House, and I felt quite embarrassed by so great a crowd of young men. It was a great treat, but I felt odd too.

Delhi, August 8, 1969

A has been unwell for some days, prob heatstroke, headaches, but has perked up and went back to school y'day. The doctor says we must keep an eye on him just in case it is the beginning of jaundice.

We have had some unbearably humid days, and everyone is feeling ghastly. TP was the perkiest of us all. Even Indians were wilting. Then we had 36 hours non-stop rain. The doctor says I must put on some weight, but I don't know how we can in this continuous Turkish-bath weather.

D's mother and I had 2 ND jaunts by scooter rickshaw, and plan more. We are getting on v well together, and I am surprised at her modern ideas—I'm far more old-fashioned on many things!

We've had Graham Forrester-Paton from Darlington to stay for a few days, and David Baker, our new Australian teacher, to dinner, v pleasant.

Y'day D had 30+ American SCMers plus some of our radical students in the sitting room—I don't know where they all sat, but it was a gt success. D is as busy as ever.

T is managing to stand, and has got more teeth. He has opened out such a lot and is v talkative.

Its v kind of Hilda and Bill Bamforth to send another parcel. They are wonderful, aren't they!

Do you remember the cream cardigan you made for me at college? Well, Sabra has pulled it out & I am going to make a jacket for A for next winter.

I went to the Coffee House with Panda for a second time, and we had a good girtlie chat –the most flippant topics you can imagine.

A gets v excited when he hears the word 'astronaut'. We have started a space scrapbook/. Tonight, he said 'People used to say the moon was made of cheese, but its really made of rocks and stones and soil". He also kmows all about aqualungs and submarines and whales and condensation. Not bad for 4½!

Delhi, August 29, 1969

You seem to be having lots of lovely days at Thornborough. I love to hear the country news & often think of that lovely little cottage.

A is now quite recovered, but, as the monsoon seems to be over, it is getting hot again, so we shall have to be careful.

TP loves to play with A and obviously adores him. A loves school, and is quite disappointed when Saturday comes. At present we have two caterpillars in jars and they have just turned into chrysalises. He is v interested in beetles, and when the garden is dug over, he spends the time squatting and watching for creatures, and then dashes in for one of us to come and look. I have had to make him a butterfly net out of an old mosquito net.

Delhi, Sept. 15, 1969

Thank you, so much, Papa, for the lovely postcards from Edinburgh.

D's mother leaves on Sunday—we have so enjoyed her stay, and I've enjoyed jaunting around with her. I look forward to showing you round again, Mama—get cracking!

We have had a fairly constant trickle, if not stream, of visitors, and D's mother has met many old friends.

I am a blood donor for the Red Cross. D arranges this among the students, and we joined in.

My big news: I have had my ears pierced! Dr. Kavan did it for me in the St Stephen's Hospital operating theatre. They look v nice with little gold studs (borrowed). [drawing—one of a woman with ornate ear-rigs, the other with washing hanging from her ears].

We have just had a parcel from Hilda and Bill, & I can't tell you how marvellous it is.

Delhi, Sept. 22, 1969

[to D's mother]

It was v thrilling but sad to see your plane go up with all the lights on. We went home immediately, and A howled in the taxi. … The house seems quite empty, and I have buried myself in all sorts of jobs to make the place feel more lively. I feel younger since your visit, and not half so drab. David Baker has been saying how he will miss you at Evening Prayer.

Today, D and A and I are going to see the new moon-landing film.

Delhi, Oct. 11, 1969

Papa's friend Mr. Patil from the Lucknow Publishing House came to tea today.

TP has taken a great leap forward—did 32 steps non-stop ... tucks into anything, fish & chips ... also asserting himself, and has a great sense of humour.

I've just made winter pyjamas for A and shirts for TP ... have knitted four sweaters and a balaclava ... I am astounded at my speed! ... lots of reading too. I'm determined to have A reading well before he starts at the British School

We had the chapel choir of 5 for a party—we now have guitars in chapel (Allan Sealy & Alexis Gilani the guitarists)– another 3 the next night, v successful, and they all claimed they had overeaten. ... also a steady stream of other visitors.

We've found somewhere to holiday next summer where the boys can enjoy themselves, at Manali in the Kulu valley—the local mission hospital doctor and his wife have set it up for us.

I now have some v pretty earrings, tiny 5-pointed star with 6 semi precious jewels of India, a traditional design from Mysore—Panda Ghose went with me to buy them. D does agree that they are an improvement on my old ears.

He went off to dig holes and mix concrete for a dispensary at a slum resettlement.

I think we've lost a lot of mail—no magazines since April.

The air now is quite cool in the morning, but we still need the fans slowly at night—the dangerous time, when everyone gets colds, though we are all well at present.

Delhi, Oct. 24, 1969

Mama, please book your flight immediately, and be here for TP's 2nd birthday on 21st March.

A loves "looking after" TP and y'day rubbed talcum powder into his hair to make him smell pretty!

A often helps D tidy away after the service in chapel, & always bows towards the altar v properly.

People say his vocabulary is fantastic. He is bi-lingual to boot, including Sabra's 'chaste' Urdu.

T is a 'rip' and always up to something.

We all 3 baked the other day, & had great fun.

Lots of knitting—I can rattle it off with a good book to read—at present Lytton Strachey on Q Vic, and lots of Delhi history, and this winter, I intend to do my own survey with camera & notebook.

I can hardly imagine an English winter & all that coldness

[drawing of family + cat = 5]

Delhi, Nov. 23, 1969

We are waiting for news of your flight, Mama.

A's eyes lit up at Papa's 'magic letter', and we soon did the tricks with suitable words. TP is blooming with health and mischief, and loves a romp with D & A. He plagues Catty.

Our winter has come and we have 2 blankets at night.

We went to see the British School new building the other day—A wanted to start immediately. An English educational trust will pay his fees.

The garden is looking good now, and we have already eaten our own veg—D has worked v hard at it.

On Sat., D took A fishing with one of our students—they caught one but were given others that we will eat tomorrow. They saw ducks, waders and kingfishers. You can imagine how thrilled A was.

Mrs. Violet Alva died suddenly on Wednesday, a great shock to the country—we saw her not so long ago.

I had arthritis again, & Dr. Natarajan got me better [request for a piece of medical equipt from UK for him]. By the way, he is mad on Andy Capp [popular UK newspaper cartoons].

We're going out to dinner with our visiting lecturer, Professor Zaehner, at Ursula & Tony King's in New Delhi [J cancelled, as T was unwell].

Delhi, Dec. 15, 1969

D went to All India Radio today with the chapel choir, recording Christmas carols. Isn't it exciting. The choir is D's brainchild and it is flourishing so well.

A's school has finished—his report, all excellent or very good, and "intelligent & cooperative ... has a very charming personality". He starts at the British Sch on 7th Jan.

D & I went shopping on behalf of Fr. Christmas, and A & I went to the Chapel carol service, while Sabra put T to bed. The choir came to the house later.

We are v pleased to hear of Barry Mackenzie's ordination D will write.

Have already made my cake—only hope the ants don't get there first. Cor, blimey what a life—anyone for ant stew with spider sauce?

Christmas … D will assist at midnight, take 6.30 at the hospital, assist at 9.30, not quite as heavy as previous years.

A to me this morning: "Wake up, tea lady. First give my favver a cuddle, then pour the tea".

I'm putting red-leaved creeper around the pictures, just like holly!

We are booked for a holiday in the hills—mountains, really—at Manali, determined to go but we know not how to find the money. There is always something turning up!

Delhi, Dec. 27, 1969

Thank you for the fabulous marvellous Selfridges parcel that arrived today.

D took A to the Crib and Carols at St James on Christmas Eve. We didn't go to the hospital service with D because it was too cold for TP so early in the morn. The boys were awake at 5.30, A jumping about saying 'He's been', so we had the stockings before D went out. A got a red scooter, & hasn't been off it since, and TP's most important to him was a polythene tea-set, and he's been having tea parties ever since.

I coped with callers during the morning, including college staff, and we had a Univ friend for lunch, and Balbir Singh (with a bottle of sherry) for supper. The Rajpals came for supper on Boxing Day, and we had lots of other callers.

Babu Lal came on Christmas morning with garlands and a cake he had made, & returned in the evening with his wife and we gave them cake & of course a little something to help out.

TP has quite a few words now, & understands everything we say. Papa, you will enjoy TP as much as A

As I write, I am on the verandah and all 3 boys are planting turnips. It is a very still afternoon, and warm, but as soon as the sun goes down after four it will get very dark and v cold.

D & I are doing a school-reader abridgement of 'David Copperfield'

We're to go out to lunch tomorrow with the Jesuits (Sabra will look after A & T)

* * * * *

1970 KULU HOLIDAY

Delhi, Jan. 11, 1970

[List of things for Mama to bring to Delhi] I do hope you will have room to bring yourself a change of clothing! Gosh, isn't it exciting!

A has now started at the British School, & on Friday he went for the first time alone. We have a very reliable regular taxi driver, Ram Singh, but A looked v small going off alone! He goes at 8 a.m., back at 1 p.m.—a very long time for a 5 yr old. He is thrilled by his own bravery, and tells the neighbours about that, and about school, with which he is also thrilled. USPG are paying his travel. We had his birthday party (for about 10) on Saturday, College servants' children.

I have had my hair cut and so back to normal … everyone approves.

I have been asked to design the costumes for Henry IViI , a rushed job.

Bitterly cold today, evidently a fresh snow fall in the Himalayas. Please bring my Tam O'Shanter for our mountain hol.

My friend from Girton, Judith Brown, is back here for a couple of months, so I will get some nice company.

Delhi, Jan. 26, 1970

I think you are both top-notch bricks! *[looking after Nana]*
So pleased you, Papa, have booked your hol in Edinburgh, and that painting commissions are rolling in.

The costumes are coming on apace, but we shall only
have them ready by the skin of our teeth. I will attend the
three performances to check the wearing of the costumes.
Then I shall start polishing and dusting for your visit!

In addition to out joint simplified version of 'David
Copperfield', D is helping Dr. Faruqi, the Professor of
Urdu, with a book, and we went for dinner there the other
night.

We've had torrential rain here. Everything was very
dusty, and now all is fresh & green— just what we needed

D plans to take A to the Beating of the Retreat again.

Mama, how will we recognise you at the airport! What
colour is your hair these days?! I have had my long, long
hair cut, & it has taken 10 years off my face. Isn't it nice, in
a few years time we shall be the same age!

Delhi, Feb. 3, 1970

[thinking Nana may have died] please get a bunch of violets
from me, just like the ones I used to take her. We are thinking & praying about you all at this time.

... bitterly cold weather—the coldest on record for the
end of January. We are all well, but taking great care.

I've been busy from dawn to dusk with play and book. We gave a performance at St. Columba's School in New Delhi, and give a schools performance tonight, and, though I shdnt say so, the costumes are a success. It was good to have more student company, and I have been asked to judge the Andrews Memorial Debate.

The boys are v excited about your visit, Tim is getting some words now. I just can't wait for you to see them.

We went for dinner at St. Stephen's Community, as Judith Brown's guests, and a quick shopping trip to ND for this and that before Granjan arrives.

Delhi, Feb. 17, 1970

[To Papa on Mama's arrival—she stayed until end of March] She's here! We had gone into College for 10 minutes this morning, & when we came back, there she was—coach from airport to New Delhi, scooter rickshaw with her luggage to our house … you could have knocked me down with a sledge hammer!

[Mama to Papa—Aidan speaks beautifully, and Tim is sweet. Juliet & Danny look v well—she's the real Juliet!

J's mother spent most of the 6 weeks at our home, and enjoying the grandsons, but had a few outings to ND with Juliet, a family picnic at the Buddha Jayanti gardens, a session with 'Mrs. Sircar's university women', and a visit to the Red Fort.]

Delhi, March 11, 1970

[to Mama in Bombay on her way home] So very sad now you are not here. You looked SO brave stepping out to the plane, but we felt rather shocked, esp when the door was closed. It seems incomplete at the moment, and your little room desolate.

Thank you for all the happy times & outings (the shops must have wondered what hit them!) Thank you for all your help & ironing. Thank you for the wonderful sewing machine, and all the wonderful things you left in the cupboards. Thank you for keeping so sprightly! Talk about 'Grannies a Go-Go'!

Delhi, April 8, 1970

[To D's mother] because he is busy as 'head examiner'.

I'm busy making A some long trousers for the hills. Norleen has given me lots of clothes for TP … and dresses for me.

Rashid *[Sabra's son]* is doing his school exams, and brings the papers for me to see. There is an excess on the school fees you gave for him, so it can go to next year.
We are paying the expenses for the Muslim equivalent of Confirmation for her children.

TP is A's shadow, and adores him, but has a v definite character of his own. He now has a few Hindi words, and A is learning Punjabi from his taxi driver.

Delhi, April 14, 1970

A is thrilled with his magic letter from Papa.

We found various things you'd accidentally left in your room. Judith Btown will bring them back to U.K.

We had Mrs. Buxton from Gainford to tea on Sunday, and are catching up on our entertaining, including the Chapel choir, and will soon be saying farewell to students leaving this year.

D is working v hard at his examinership—the temp is now 103 and all the flowers are dying off and we pulled out the sweetpeas this morning. There are bunches and bunches of grapes.

Went to a leprosy settlement with some American ladies —I hope to do some designing of things they weave.

I wish you cd see A & TP in the afternoons—they block up the drain with a towel in your bathroom and turn on the tap—they manage to get 3" of water before it floods out of the front door. They spend an hour like that every day to keep cool.

Amrita came round with some ear-rings for you! Panda & I went to the coffee house and we had a good chat the other day.

We are sleeping on the verandah—lovely fresh air, down to about 80 at night, though it could get up to about 97! We are all looking forward to Manali, & everything is geared to that.

A loves school, and TP has lots more words—he sings beautifully in Chapel with a very deep voice!

Delhi, May 1, 1970

We have been in a flat spin this last few weeks:- as head examiner, D has 16 examiners—each has to see him 3 times —the house is a cross between a railway station and a non-stop café, and it's been up to 110.

We've also been catching up on some entertaining. Our American friends, the Sheltons, came for a farewell dinner recently, and another family for tea, and 8 boys in for a big supper. On Tues, 2 lecturers for lunch, and we went out for dinner. Y'day, Mrs. Sircar came for coffee and both for dinner, and Nette and Faruqi one evening, and next week we have 3 engagements booked, including the Bengali head of economics & Mrs. Ray.

From next term, A will have 2 more little boys in his taxi. That will be quite a sight. At school, he says he only plays with 'the bashers'. TP loves the stars and the moon, and asks to go out to see then if he is ever still awake.

Just D and me and the boys and David Baker at the last eucharist of term.

D has just sold his Eliot book, so we have no worries for the hol.

Himalaya Guest House (Gulab Das koti) Manali, Kulu, May 20, 1970

What a lot of adventures I have to tell you!

On Sunday 17th, we caught the 8.45 bus—6 hours to Chandigarh. With Delhi at 116, the journey was rather hot. Our arrangements for the night had fallen through, but we found a hotel "The Aroma" ! to take us, a nice room with a private bathroom—within minutes, the boys were in the shower. In the evening, we took a scooter-rickshaw tour of the city, where D had been before, and he showed us all the main, magnificent Le Corbusier buildings

That night, we had a wonderful Indian dinner … a call at 6 a.m., our plane for Kulu took off at 8.45. We had a marvellous view of the Himalayas, but, over Kulu the plane had to turn back (mist had made it too dangerous to land), so, back to Ch. There we met a New Zealand lady also trying to reach the Himalaya Guest House, so we agreed to share a taxi with her at great expense! We hastily collected food and water, and set out at 1 p.m. It was very hot, and we were all parched—I have never drunk so many coca colas as that day! Our lips were swollen & cracked, and TP's were bleeding. As night fell, we were on single-track mountain roads, with overhanging cliffs, and the raging torrent of the River Beas below—it was hair-raising, but fortunately by this time both boys were asleep. I was terrified, and the driver had to be told to slow down … by 11.30, we reached Kulu, and found a nice little hotel, and we all, NZ lady included, slept in the one room—everyone was very obliging, and the next morning we caught a very crowded and colourful local bus to Manali—the local women all with lots of rings in their ears, the men with Kulu caps, like the one I sent you, Daddy. At Manali, we got coolies to carry the luggage. We called at the CMS Hospital for some groceries, and then up the mountain to this gorgeous little doll's house, the dearest little house you can imagine, neat and clean.

We are cooking for ourselves on a kerosene stove.

We went down to the little town today for shopping, and the climb back, 2,000 feet. nearly killed us! TP has a carrying chair (made for us in Kamla Nagar) on D's back, and I carried a rucksack of groceries—phew!

Others in the NZ party here include 2 children, 3 & 4, so they are all v happy together, and there is a stream by the side door for them to play in.

Now we are all set for a wonderful hol.

Manali, May 28, 1970

Thank you for a p.c. from Edinburgh, your favourite city.

Quite unable to tell you how magnificent it all is, surrounded by the eternal snows, pine and oak forests, terraced rice and barley fields, apple orchards, waterfalls, buttercups and daisies, the interesting hill people, and herds of goats. At this time of year, shepherds bring their flocks a hundred miles from the Kangra valley to the uplands. The house has orchards and a farm—Aidan and TP spend a great deal of time with the little cows and their calves (a small mountain breed), and drinking tea with Gulab and Mrs. Das in the farmhouse. They provide us fresh milk every day, and jars of jam and honey. D now goes down to do the shopping.

Everyone is hungry all the time. I am eating things I haven't eaten for months, and we are all growing fat and rosy.

Today, we took our food and pans up the mountain and made a fire—in what we are calling Dingley Dell—and had bacon, tomatoes, onions, bread and tea, v v delicious, and when we got back, TP asked for lunch and ate 4 dishes of cornflakes.

Tomorrow, D is going to try for trout in the Beas.

There are glow worms here, with bright green head-lamps at night.

I wish you cd see us setting off for a picnic, T riding in his chair, me with rucksack, and A with nothing. The other day, TP insisted on walking a very long way up a mouintain and loved it. We are all enjoying the freedom, and the privacy. Sorry this is such a self-centred letter, but am v eager to tell you about this wonderful place & our holiday.

There is an electricity strike, so we are sharing the hurricane lamp to write our letters.

Manali, June 18, 1970

One week left. We are writing this by candle-light, as no electricity tonight.

A spends a lot of time in the farm kitchen, chatting in Hindi, and they let him & T feed the cows. Their dog comes with us when we go on picnics. I am learning to milk a cow! I thought it would be a useful thing to learn. I manage about a cup in 5 minutes.

... a wonderful picnic last week, a three-hours walk on a path up the mountain through woods of pine, chestnut and walnut. I have never been in such a foresty forest. We met several cowherds and shepherds and woodcutters. We had quite a chat with one of the woodcutters, who told us there were bears about. When we came to our picnic place, he went away whistling loudly (if you know it is bear country, whistle or sing as loud as you can so as not to startle them). A walked very well, but was a bit frightened and kept breaking into loud song and persuading us all to do likewise. We had lovely views of the snows above and the foaming river far below.

A couple of times, we have been to a wood nearby, with a small temple, with a goddess without whose approval local festivities cannot take place. ... it is supposed to be a v sinister place.

Now is the time when the terraces are flooded and the rice planted. A waded in and helped a lady planting, while T sat on the farmer's knee!

D has had a few fishing trips, unsuccessful, with one of our students and his father, staying nearby. He enjoys the blue sweater you knitted for him.

We all went with D when he went to celebrate HC at the hospital one Sunday.

We have had several lovely riverside picnics with sheltered shingle beaches and sandy bits—lots of pretty stones, too.

Today, we were taken to the hot sulphur baths at a village with lovely carved-wood houses. There is a bath for the men, the water going on to the one for the women. There is also a paying bath that we went to, separate pipe line, blue tiled—we had a family bath, great fun. We felt marvellous afterwards, and fantastically clean.

The villagers were busy threshing corn with animals on the threshing floor and winnowing the grain in the wind.

I am doing a bit of sketching, and enjoying it enormously. The boys are imps, and the other night, I found potatoes in my sleeping bag!. They had a glow worm for a pet y'day, and a tadpole today.

Delhi, July 8, 1970

We have been tremendously busy since we got back.

Here is my account of our journey home after the most wonderful holiday ever. Gulab Das was in tears at A's going. The Snells at the hospital put us up for our last night to save us a dash down the hill at dawn. We got a bus from Manali to Kulu at 6.30 a.m. and eventually arrived at the airport— landing strip is more accurate, and you have to be pretty nifty to get airborne and miss the mountains. After hours waiting, it was announced—no plane— bad weather. The airline got us a funny hotchpotch lunch from the bazaar, and after many delays put us in the little airline bus to Chandigarh. The driver was excellent and the bus v good on the corners etc, but I was almost ill with fright, and had to change my seat! We stopped at one or two springs to cool the bus radiator, and then had 'high tea' v quickly at Bilaspur and bashed on to Chandigarh for 11.30 p.m. I leapt off the bus and dashed to the hotel & was lucky enough to bag the last room—far from clean but better than the bus station. We were up at dawn & D went off to book bus seats to Delhi. After b'fast, the bus left at 8.30 a.m., and we reached Delhi at 3 p.m. I can't tell you how wonderful it was to be home again—everywhere was so clean, and a meal was ready.

Since then, we've had the water cut off several days, and both boys have had rather severe flu, high temperatures & violent shivers, but Dr. Natarajan has been and they are recovering—though there was no electricity—no fans—for 9 hours on their worst day. The monsoon broke on the Monday after the Saturday when we arrived, so we keep having showers to cool us a bit, and I put both patients on a bed on the verandah one afternoon. Catty has not left us since we returned—at night, on D's pillow, then mine, then my feet—we thought he would burst with purring.

A starts school again on Wed., and I am busy preparing his clothes, and have a meeting with the Mums of the boys who will share the taxi.

We had a nice end-of-vacation trip to ND, to a Rajasthan handicrafts exhibition, with refreshments at Wenger's afterwards. We bought a jolly little picture, and D bought me a sweet little necklace, topaz and amethysts—doesn't it sound exotic—that just a fortnight after a lovely Kulu shawl ... now back to reality, a huge income tax demand.

We've had a HUGE scorpion in the sitting room. Catty spotted it, and D killed it with A's cricket bat. We also had a centipede about 7" long—this is the season for such creatures—ugh!

Well, life now seems to be fairly well organised—shall soon be making jam, and the tapestry is coming on quite quickly.

The students arrive on Tuesday.

Delhi, July 20, 1970

Congratulations Mama … President, Stockton Business and Professional Women!

Aidan and TP have both had bouts of fever, but Dr. N has seen them. At school last week, A got one red and five gold stars—we are all terribly proud … he has gone up into the 2nd class, another cause of pride! TP has lots of words.

Two of Sabra's children were in hospital briefly, but we managed.

The weather is ghastly, the monsoon in suspense … hideously humid, and as I say to D, you wake up as if you have been sleeping in the frying pan.

D was away last weekend taking a retreat at Kanpur, but now term has started and soon life will be in its old hectic routine.

We are busy trying to work out how long to stay here—we are due on leave in 1971 but will pbby need to wait until 1972. How we shall ever settle down in UK, I do not know, but no doubt God will take care of all that, also where. We are not anxious, but a bit curious. Right now, I'd like a move to the Arctic.

All 4 of us went to Romesh Bhattacharji, ex-chapel pianist's wedding to Shobana Mukarji on Saturday at the Cathedral, and on to the reception at the Ashoka, so we did get cooled down a bit. *[Shobhana became a teacher at Jesus and Mary College, and Romesh became Narcotics Commissioner for India]*

Delhi, August 25, 1970

We have agreed a definite extension to 1972. It will be a tremendous wrench to leave … we just believe the right job will make itself obvious as did this one. I think A will find UK very odd … he saw a tv in a shop—"what's that funny thing? he asked.

[J unwell, concussion, playing with T—"he never felt a thing!"— 3 weeks recovering] We kept my birthday and our 7th anniversary 'at home'. Dr. Natarajan has looked after me very carefully.

We all 4 went to lunch the other day at Prof Faruqi's.

I am doing textile designs for the leprosy centre workers, and costumes for a one-act version of Sheridan directed by Allan Sealy.

Mary Earnshaw is on her way back here from UK, having decided the nun's life is not for her. We're hoping to go to Palam to meet her.

TP is a real little imp these days—he now has 303 words —he'd be happy for me to read to him all morning. D & I went to a parent's evening at A's school to be introduced to the 'new maths'—he will have 2 afternoons at school this winter, to do such interesting things as acting, drama, art, music, sport, etc.

Delhi, Sept. 4,1970

I have recovered just in time, for I have been given 3 plays to do. The first is Fratti's *Che* for 18th Sept ff, Then the Marovitz *Hamlet* for 8th Oct ff., with stylized costumes and masks and mod-ed dance movements—I'm looking fwd to it! And the Shakespeare Soc's production, *Twelfth Night*, first week in Nov *[postponed to Jan]*—phew! Have also been asked to coach in speech for *Macbeth*, and, when that is over, to coach the College debaters—never knew my English Speaking Union diploma would be so useful!

Am now making a new dress on the machine and have material for shirts for Aidan—he's been to two parties of late and am going to make him a special shirt for them now. TP is talking like mad now. The boys often talk about you —in glowing terms!

Last night, D & I went to a cocktail party to say farewell to our only New Delhi friends, the Kings —something more rollicking, or at least younger is more in my line—hey ho!

Have now been asked to help with our College boys' production of 'You're a good man, Charlie Brown' for television. Its nice to feel wanted!

Looking fwd to a full account of Edinburgh.

Delhi, Sept. 18, 1970

Thank you for such a full letter, rcvd y'day morn, and for the glorious and unusual Edinburgh view. Yes I wd like to go all round the city with you Papa, one day.

D is sending an engraving to Papa, and we hope he will do a painting from it in time for our homecoming in 1972.

I'm learning from Allan Sealy to play the guitar—we had been saving for a dog, but are to be <u>given</u> one *[missing letter? We had had a bad burglary and needed a watchdog]* we decided the money could be used on this ambition. Apart from my own interest, I am very keen to foster music in A & TP. They now both play it and sing—you should hear them!

Delhi, Sept. 24, 1970

The first play is over. I had a curtain call, and went on to take my bow, wearing v mod Indian clothes !! Also presented with a gorgeous bouquet, then to the cast party with D, which was all great fun.

We are now the proud owners of a beautiful white Lhasa apso ('terrier') called Bhai—a genuine Tibetan, pure bred —for a watchdog. D, of all people, is completely gone on her. An American friend, going home, was looking for a home for her, and she has settled perfectly with us. D found her on the bed the other day, and didn't murmur, and later explained. "Well. she is such a lovely clean dog!" She is used to kids mauling her, but won't let anyone else near the house day or night. Sleeps by my bed, and follows me like a shadow.

Her former owner also gave me a huge bundle of clothes —gorgeous things outgrown by her teenage daughter— which I have been busy altering.

A's age group no longer have afternoon school—they were all crying with tiredness. They will try again when it is cooler. He plays here with the local boys, Jagat and Cheti etc., in the afternoons.

He woke D the other morning, whistling loudly, 'I'm whistling with happiness'.

We all 4 had an outing to the zoo, only 1d each to get in, being World Wildlife Week.

Am writing to Janet & Sylvia.

We've booked a holiday at Gulab Das' for next summer, and he's reduced the price for us!

I got fantastic praise in the student newspaper for my Marowitz Hamlet costumes! And I'm reading Percy Spear's 'Twilight of the Mughals' (Percy taught here long ago, D writes to him at Cambridge)

Delhi, Nov. 26, 1970

… long silence, after an awful illness *[dengue—both J and D]* … it was ghastly but we are now fully recovered.

It is really winter here, now, and I am knitting like mad, sweaters for A and TP.

209

The Snells from Manali came to see us, with all the Kulu news, and brought a huge box of apples for A from Gulab Das.

Two Gazettes arrived today, and the Giles Cartoons—which Dr. Natarajan can't wait to read.

Bhai is now very beautiful and healthy, and has put on a very luxurious white winter coat.

I'm just getting "Twelfth Night" launched for January.

All 4 of us went to the circus—and then we paid for Sabra and family and the sweeper and family to go. Aidan loved one particularly disgusting (his word) clown.

D & I went to a lovely open day at the British School—A has come on "in leaps and bounds", quoting his teacher. His writing is now very firm and he has speeded up, so he finishes his work. He is full of ideas, and his factual inform-ation is tremendous—you should hear Elspeth *[Shankland]* of all people, praising him—also fluent in Hindustani! Can't you see me swelling with pride! He used the word 'normal' the other day, and, asked what he meant, said "Well, you've heard of abnormal, haven't you? This is normal"

TP is full of funny sayings ... vocab v large, and long sentences.

Mary was here for supper the other night, and D & I went to dinner at Fr. Byron's last night (now Vicar at St James, Kash Gate). A & TP went to a party at the rich fam-ily's house in Cavalry Lines.

Delhi, Dec. 8, 1970

What lovely snaps of you ready for the wedding, Mummy—looking like the Dowager Duchess of Dacca or the Hon Mrs. Plonk. Also liked the photo of your ladies jaunt to Eastbourne—but what a dreadful row of middle-aged knees! (Yours are OK)

Have made my C Cake early this year, and finished knitting sweaters (just socks to do) so have time for the guitar. Have just started designing the costumes for 'Twelfth Night'.

When we were ill, I missed judging the inter-colleges debate—the other judges were editor of a national newspaper, and drama critic of another, I was of course to supply the glamour, I don't think!

Janet has written to ask me to be godmother to her second baby, due in February—could you be proxy, Mama?

We all went to tea with Nirupam Sen's parents—also a supper party at Romesh and Shobhana Bhattacharji's

Kenneth Jennings, vice-principal of Cuddesdon, is coming to lunch tomorrow

T has grown 6" since last Manali, by his trousers.

A is longing, longing for a magic letter, Granpa! He is in the school carol choir along with the American, German and Japanese Schools.

Gulab Das has reduced the price at Manali for us next year! V decent.

I've inherited Evelyn's bike, so I'm off to post this at the PO.

Delhi, Dec. 16, 1970

[Thanks for parcel brought by Denys de la Hoyde, including medical items requested by Dr. Natarajan] a great sack of goodies, wonderful, wonderful things

On Sunday, went to the Cathedral with D for the unification of ministries—D is now a presbyter of the Church of North India with all the other Anglicans, most Bapts, Meths. etc. It was a tremendously awe-inspiring service, and v well organised. We also had Holy Communion, all 1,300 of us. That evening, Mary sat, so we cd go to the Old Students' Dinner.

On Tuesday, Denys and D and I went to dinner at the Brotherhood.
Nette & Prof Faruqi to tea.

D is transplanting turnips and I am having guitar practice

Fri was Founders Day, and I was able to attend HC in chapel followed by b'fast in the college. Café ... candlelit dinner on the front lawn, then, later, wonderful Shakespeare bits by a group of professional actors from UK. ... must start baking for Christmas—what a day!

[It is impossible to remember when we reached the conclusion that we should do just two tours in India. We were due on leave in 1971, but, in view of Mr. Sircar's retirement, due in April 1972, we agreed with the Bishop to stay on until his successor was in place. That that should be the terminus was not easy to accept, especially as we came under intense pressure from the new Principal to return after leave in 1972. One question was the future, not least the educational future of A&TP, another, as time went on, was the health of D's sister in U.K. and our wish to be nearer to her in what we discovered was a terminal illness, but almost until we set off in May 1972, we agonised about whether to return]

* * * * *

Delhi, Jan. 14, 1971

... only one day off, 25h Dec ... I and the boys made a 'jugghi' Christmas crib for the Chapel carol service ... I was extremely busy with Christmas, and the play immediately after, and have been in bed with a bad dose of flu. We had so many callers, we were just about screaming by the start of the play on 4th Jan —a choir of about 50 Naga students came and sang carols in our house. My Polish friend Martha Guha spent Christmas Day with us

Just can't imagine your snow. The first winter back will be fantastic for the boys.

'Twelfth Night' went v well—I had already caught flu, but took my bow when called for. The party was to be in a local disco—I did not think D wd enjoy that (in fact, he said he wd have gone for me), so I declined—2 days later, a beautiful Interflora bouquet and a lovely iced cake inscribed 'Thank you' arrived. And a lovely note from the cast— wasn't that sweet of them. "To repeat our thanks and to say how much we all missed you at the party". I was absolutely thrilled ... I designed Sir Andrew Aguecheek's wig, and had to fit it every night—what a giggle—and I made all the Elizabethan ruffs.

[urges Papa to come for a holiday—Baked beans are available here! I'd love to show you round my Delhi— but he declined]

Your magic letter (with the jumping paper clips) has disappeared from my dressing table. Such is our sweeper's 'tidying'. I'm almost driven bats by his particular peculiarity.

We all 4 went to the Republic Day parade—and the tribal dancing.

D had to go to a conference at Patiala, so Mary came and stayed with us. D made quite an impression, and I feel v proud of him

Delhi, Feb. 17, 1971

Since 'Twelfth Night', we have had 'Caligula' by Camus, and that was all togas and tunics. The dersi couldn't come, so I had to sew most of them. Most of the cast were freshers, & they did v well. At the end, I was called to the stage and presented with a lovely art book and a rose!—Great fun, and a lovely party at a ND 'cellar' later. Mary baby sat for us.

A has been v poorly with a chesty cough, but Dr. N soon put him right.

D went to Nirupam Sen's wedding at Patna, so Mary came again. The following Sunday, D & I went to the reception at the Ashoka. The bridegroom is just off to Moscow as third secretary.

On another afternoon, we went to a reception for Red Cross blood donors at Rashtrapati Bhavan, with the President, Dr. Giri—D does work v hard to get donors but did not expect to get invited to such a thrilling event … he was presented with a certificate for "humane services" We were later able to greet the President personally.

[We had attended an identical occasion some years previously, in 1966, not in Juliet's letters, when we met President Radhakrishnan]

At present we have David Gosling staying for approx 5 weeks—he is working in Bangalore, but has come to Delhi for part of his research.

Went to a smart wedding reception (lecturer) in New Delhi ... and last night to dinner with the organist of St. James, Louis Joseph.

Papa's friends Mr. & Mrs. Nicholls have had us over to their flat in ND, and they are coming here.

Today I am having an Ashoka morning (making use of A's school taxi) ... my 'hairdo'.

Last Sunday, a big SCM do in College—the chapel music was v good.

My guitar playing is definitely making strides, but unfortunately my teacher is busy with his exams.

The boys are prize pranksters. Tim's vocabulary is fantastic & he gets v funny ideas—can't believe he will be 3 this month.

I've taken up badminton again—I play with the state champion, a student, and enormously enjoy it.

D had an unexpected day off last week, so he and T & I piled into a scooter rickshaw, picked up Aidan from school, and had a picnic in the Buddha Jayanti gardens.

4th March—sorry to tell you, A has measles, very ill and delirious! Dr. Natarajan is coping very well. I'm just waiting for TP to start.

Am once again sleeping on the floor—neck pains etc.

Have just finished Fair Isle sweater and bobble cap for TP in Manali, and must start the same for A.

For last week's Brotherhood garden party, D & I went half and half because of A's illness.

Am having Janet, the hosp. dietician, to stay for a couple of days, so we will have a good girls' time.

Delhi, April 15, 1971

Congratulations, Papa, at your BBC contract, and your ballet music on the radio.

It has been up to 104, but we have had dust storms & it has cooled down.

D and I went to a lovely recital in ND—soprano, cello, harpsichord—and to the High Commission's latest play, and then on for coffee.

Baking hard for 25 students—all D's honours class who are leaving come to tea tomorrow.

A is going to another party tomorrow—in his school taxi (the little snob!).
Both boys are fully recovered and bouncing. A was boasting that he was brave enough to touch a tiger, or a

lion, or a leopard. "Or a monkey?" says Tim. "Begorrah and bejabers", said A, "I'd just say that to a monkey"—and he snapped his fingers. I could hardly keep a straight face.

Dr. Christanand for lunch.

A says his teacher, Miss Pegg, is "Very lovely—she loves everyone, even the children".

D has just been paid a nice cheque for his book of plays, so we have got our fare to Manali.—can't wait to get there —shall do lots more sketching … fresh spring water to drink, picnics, camp fires—wippeee. Bhai, our dog, will come, too, and will surely love the mountains as a Tibetan

Delhi, April 18, 1971

One of our favourite students, my guitar teacher, Allan Sealy, has got a scholarship to Michigan, a very good friend and a very talented boy. On the guitar, I can now play the tunes of quite a few Sidney Carter songs.

We are preparing for Manali—y'day, bought two anoraks—we will pbby have to go the whole way by bus as flights seem uncertain.

A & TP have both been ill—same old flu' —they do get these 36 hour things, all very tropical.

Our annual staff dinner the other night—as boring as usual—ladies at one side gentlemen at the other, as usual. Also went to dinner at the hospital the other night, not much fun either. We all need a holiday.

Have just finished warm pyjamas for the boys at Manali.

A friend from the Bengal border is coming for the day, so we'll hear about the refugees.

Delhi, May 3, 1971

This is only to enquire about your health Mama. Letters are taking 8-10 days.

I've just had an air-conditioned morning at the Ashoka, getting my hair cut before our holiday. Mary Earnshaw will join us for a fortnight at Manali.

Y'day evening, Parent Teachers Association at the British Schjool, always very worthwhile, and dinner at the Brotherhood.

Delhi, May 13, 1971

Birthday Greetings to Mama & Papa.

I have been dashing between home & hospital, where D has been recovering from an op for a strangulated hernia. Dr. N diagnosed it on Sunday evening, and whipped him into Tirath Ram Hospital and a well-known surgeon operated on Monday morn … today he is looking much better—he'll be there about 10 days. I had to stay two nights, as they could not provide a night attendant. We blame the hernia on the kick-start on the scooter, which we've decided we'll have to sell now.

With the doctor's permission, we'll hope to fly to Manali.

Dr. N wants to know how much money he has with you, because he wants to buy some more surgical instruments.

Manali, June 4, 1971

At last, we are here ! The flight from Delhi on the 27th was cancelled … at vast expense, we hired a taxi. What a journey ! On the way across Punjab, somewhere near Rupar, the driver, Ram Singh, took us off across field tracks to his family village, where we had a wonderful reception, the old mother and father and all the family, and a great meal had been prepared for us—delicious omelettes, hot milk, sweets, ghee. We admired the baby, and took every-one's photograph. It was a delightful interlude, and we felt very honoured.

All went well up the twisty road until the Ghastly Gorge — there had been much unseasonal rain, lots of landslides, and between Kulu and Manali the road had been washed away completely and we were driving over rubble and wet, slippery sand close to the river. We were v frightened, but the driver was v careful. By then, it was pitch dark … we got here about 8.30 p.m., having left home at 3.45 a.m. D had been fine on the journey, but was exhausted and not v well the next day.

Since then, we have just pottered until we get up strength to do things. The boys caught 11 tadpoles today, and I have been down the terrible hill shopping, D being unable to carry anything. The countryside is as glorious as ever… birds, including hawks hunting, & a cuckoo …there is a myna nesting under the eaves by our window … on the opposite hillside, we watched shepherds from Kangra with their flocks looking for somewhere to camp *[description of their clothes, with drawing]*—thick homespun white wool, the top is bloused, & they often carry a lamb in it, the skirt is short, very full—Greek-looking. Legend has it that they are descended from Alexander's army.

Manali, June 20, 1971

Y'day, I received Papa's letter from Edinburgh, posted on 27th May!

We've had the worst June in 53 years in the Kulu valley with an early monsoon and landslides all over the place, with no road access into Kulu some of the time —but some glorious sunshine this past few days.

A & TP spent a morning knee deep in the paddy fields planting rice with the local farmer—they were thrilled to be allowed to help … I took A and a friend down to a water mill (each is in a small stone hut and looked after by a woman), and they were fascinated to watch the flour being ground.

Gulab Das has given me a spinning bodkin—this winter I have great plans for craft work.

Tomorrow, A says he is going to help Gulab Das prop up his apple trees—there is such a fabulous crop that the branches need supporting.

We are having a wonderful holiday —I am enjoying the cooking, too, and hauling the rations up the mountain is not too bad.

Re returning to UK (next April?), we just feel the right job will become so obvious that it will be silly to refuse, just as this one was.

Delhi, July 17, 1971

We had a good holiday, but I was glad to get back for a rest. It was a long way up with the shopping!

The Young Scientists Club sounds terrific, Papa. A wondered why the newspaper called you Mr. Wood, when your name is 'Granpa' !

The journey down was fantastic
We set off by bus at 5 a.m. To Kulu was fine, and we only had to cross rivers twice where the bridge was washed away—we were the last bus out of Manali for 4 days! At Kulu, it started to rain, and poured all day. It took 9 1/2 hours through the Ghastly Gorge instead of 1 1/2. Waterfalls were hammering onto the road, breaking it up ... the road was littered in many places with fallen rocks, and there were several gangs clearing landslides. Eventually we came on a bulldozer, which took an hour to clear one fall, & then we crept along behind it, and caught up on a convoy of cars, another bus and some tankers ... the road is narrow and twisty and was just churned mud... stuff was falling all the time ... this went on for hours and hours. Below, the Beas was in spate. Eventually, we came to a fall with huge boulders, where the road was completely blocked. At this point, we climbed over the landslide with the boys and our luggage and Bhai, and exchanged passengers with another bus that had been trying to come up the way, and reached Mandi at 5.30 p.m. A special night bus was put on for Chandigarh, which we reached at 3 a.m. ... 5.15 a.m. to

222

Delhi, in time for lunch, in all about 30 hours! I used to think Whitby was the end of the world !

Since then, we have been v busy preparing for school and college, and throwing out accumulated junk in preparation for leaving next year. We have got a definite booking for 4th April, Bombay to Genoa, then train.

I've arranged for Tim to go to the nursery school in September—can you imagine that ! A is back at school and getting on well with reading at last.

D is progressing well, but gets v uncomfortable with prolonged sitting or teaching.

I've found a wonderful 'nearly new' clothes place, and am stocking up for next year. I'm afraid Mama will find me very dowdy in my 2nd hand clothes next year.

Delhi, August 5, 1971

Thank you both for lovely letters.

We've started the drama season early this year, and my first play, 'Charley's Aunt' starts on 19th August, late Victorian but I am putting it in 1918-22 style costumes, with Victorian furniture borrowed from St Stephen's Community house—also helping with production. I've also been asked to do 'The Merchant of Venice' in December, and there may be more in between. I'm doing some of the sewing to save the Society's money. Also doing speech and breathing exercises, and hoping to learn some Indian arts and crafts to bring to teach somewhere in UK.

We've bought 'for England' a lovely Kashmere work-box, which I've lined with dark blue velvet—you'll love it! … also a 'silver' jug and glasses. Lots of people have asked for our worldly goods, so I have made a list (we've sold the scooter to David Frey's father, a brigadier in the army), and spent a happy morning in the bazaar buying brass pans and hope to get some cotton carpets—namdas

Talking of woodpeckers to Tim, "yes, and baby pickers". Aidan is using words like 'transfer' and is v fond of sums.

Delhi, August 30, 1971

'Charley's Aunt' was a <u>huge</u> success, & everyone said the costumes were a fantastic wow! The Snells from Manali came on the last night, their last night in India!

I'm working on 'The Royal Hunt of the Sun' for 24th September, about the Spanish conquest of Peru … involves fabulous Inca masks. I've done the designs and will start work tomorrow.

I'm to judge, with one other, a two-day drama competition in College.

With some of the scooter money, we've bought for our homecoming some fabulous cotton carpets and a brass table.

Hope to soon get organised to collect all my Delhi Mutiny data—no, not to publish, just an heirloom. I've now read about 10 books on the topic and started my photographic record. Have just finished a book on Havelock—incredible man—seven horses shot from under him! *[a stu-*

dent, Ashok Nath, later to be an admired military historian, took up from Juliet the idea of photographing the '1857' sites]

I also plan this winter, between plays, to learn favourite Indian cookery from staff wives, also batik & lacquer work. The rest of the time is for darning and ironing!

For my birthday D and A took me to a lovely dance drama about Krishna followed by chicken curry at Moti Mahal—A was nearly asleep t'ards the end, but v thrilled to be up late. A few days later, D & A and I went with Benji Gilani to the cinema to see 'My Fair Lady' our third visit to the cinema in our time in Delhi!

Tim starts nursery school on Wednesday and is v excited—he was complaining the other day that his bottom teeth were upside down.

How was dear old Edinburgh this time? Aidan wants to join your Young Scientists club, Granpa.

At the Bishop's request, we are delaying our departure until a sailing at the end of May, now Bombay to Venice, then train, arriving UK early July. The Sircars retire at end of April.

Delhi, Oct. 18, 1971

At the end of last term, we both felt v tired, so we all went to Simla for a last look—it did us all good to have some good mountain air with lovely views of the snows, our last of the Himalayas—and country walks and picnics with the Gilani brothers, and a very pleasant luncheon party at the home of another student at Summerhill. TP & A had pony rides, and we have a carved walking stick for you, Papa. I got some Chinese shoes made (the last pair were a dream to wear), and picked up a few necklaces ! Aidan made a book of 28 pressed flowers, 24 of which we identified. We were away for a week—I had intended to write from Simla, but was always too tired. On the homeward bus, a man sitting beside us got off, and another man got on. TP: "That boy has growed into someone else."

A is full of schoolboy jokes—its awful!

We went to a friend's wedding reception the other night.

Today is Diwali, and we let off the fireworks with great excitement all round, and have little oil lamps around the house, and it looks v pretty.

Congrats, Papa, on your membership of the Edinburgh Astronomical Society—will give you even more of a feeling of belonging to that glorious city.

We've just put in our veg seeds, and they were up in 3 days—it will be v different in UK!

Must go and knit, the cold weather being upon us (I've made three blankets from old sweaters.

I still do practically all my shopping in Kamla Nagar, nobody stares at me and I feel really at home there.

Delhi, Dec. 4,1971

We are very well and v safe. *[Indo-Pak confrontation and liberation of Bangladesh]* From last night, we have a blackout as a precaution. Today, we heard the siren twice, but nothing came over here. Yesterday, there was bombing in Srinagar, Agra & Ambala, and today, Pak officially declared war. Please do not worry—there is nothing to worry about.

I am v busy with 'The Merchant of Venice'—presumably 'the show will go on'. It is rather sad, as this will be my last one here.

For weeks, we've had callers every evening—often 4 or 5 boys—the amount of coffee and sugar that has flowed through the house! Life is one long snack bar.

A is practising for the big carol-singing gathering in the American school—and TP is learning all sorts of delightful little Hindi action songs at school.

D is dashing about all over as usual. I am doing talks etc with the Debating Society, and knitting, crocheting, tapestry, water colours. Also clearing the house over and over to reduce our possessions—all part of the packing process. The white ants have eaten all but 3 of our original tea chests, so we are having to buy tin trunks.

We are using all our blankets and quilts as the air at night is very keen. Whatever will we do this time next year?!

Thank you for the newspapers which trickle in. I haven't had a 'Woman & Home' for months.

Today we went to a lovely exhibition of Delhi crafts, and came home with a lovely little Tibetan painting. Recently we went to dinner with Romesh & Shobhana Bhattacharji, and another day with Nirupam's parents.

From now until Monday, I shall be submerged in the play, after that, Christmas (we've had a wonderful Selfridge's parcel from Bill and Hilda), and then down the homeward slope—what a strange feeling all that will be.

Do tell us all about the snow—T & A wd love to hear, & so would I—drop a line in between shovelling loads of it Whatever will we do, this time next year?

Delhi, Dec. 15, 1971

We've just heard on the radio that Dacca has surrendered, so let's hope it will all soon be over. ... In Delhi, all is normal, except no evening weddings, and notices against hoarding.

Tuesday was Founder's Day in College, including an art exhibition ... some very talented boys ... we bought a painting by one of them, and one by our Bursar, Deejan Ghose. You can see us in the UK without a stick of furniture, but w wonderful paintings.

Well, the play went off very well—the production was excellent and the costumes were much admired. It was a very nice one to finish with, but, as you can imagine, a rather sad feeling for me. You will no doubt enjoy reading comments written in all my programmes from the plays.

Today I went off to a 'speaking engagement' (ahem) in another college in the University, Miranda House !! It was hugely enjoyed, and 'very interesting'—although I shdnt tell you all that. I go for my second talk on Friday. Rather jumping on the family bandwagon! Its been alarming to find how much I enjoy standing up and gassing. [numbers went up at the 2nd talk, and all members of the Eng Dept staff were present] There will be more there, too, next term. And tomorrow, I am again judging at the College debating society.

Now I must prepare for Christmas—A is cutting out angels and stars for the mobile.

Chrysanths are all out now.

Delhi, Dec. 18, 1971

On the evening of the surrender of Dacca, a crowd went round the Univ shouting 'Jai Bangla' & 'Indira Gandhi zindabad' etc., and tonight the blackout has been lifted. There are hundreds wounded & killed & it seems so much more tragic when it has been such a short war.

I've changed round the sitting-room furniture so we can sit round the fire. It is very cosy!

Today, we went to an end of term concert at Tim's school—he was Jack in 'Jack & Jill' *[details of school report—all subjects vgood]* … cooperative and intelligent … after the concert, we went to the College Café for an end of term treat.

[details of A's report from Miss Pegg] "a dear little boy, he is happy, self-disciplined and obedient, and progressing nicely". I am afraid he is going like a lot of European children who live for a length of time in the tropics. He is very thin, and pale, and peaky-looking and has not much energy. School really does tire him out, quite drastically. He does get vitamins and malt and milk and rest—I think there is

very little we can do until we get those wonderful sea breezes next year. He's had a lot of fevers these last few months, and he really needs a break from this climate. Don't cry, Mama—I will take care of both of them!

Today, A &TP & I made mincemeat in preparation for the 25th, and checked over the Christmas tree. Maybe next year we will have a real one!

D has been offered wonderful jobs [in Delhi and Lahore]. No doubt something will turn up in UK soon! He and I went shopping on behalf of Father Christmas y'day.

* * * * *

INTERLUDE 'Mushaira'

[The reference on 15th Dedcember to the end of the Indo-Pak war which saw East Pakistan become Bangladesh introduces a piece Juliet wrote about a 'celebratory' event at the Lal Qila (the Red Fort) that we were taken to by our friend, Professor Khwaja Ahmad Faruqi]

One of the most moving events I have ever witnessed in India was an open-air poetry reading. Called a 'mushaira', it is a traditional Muslim form of entertainment which can be enjoyed by all castes and classes. The mushaira we attended was set against the backcloth of the Lal Qila, the Red Fort of Delhi, the old mughal palace of a long line of proud rulers.

The white marble glittered in the moonlight, and, futther off, domes and minarets made a romantic silhouette against the deep blue sky. Through the sculptured archways and delicately carved stone screens, it was easy to imagine the drifting muslin of courtesans glimpsed for a moment as they slipped quickly back to the harem. It did not require much imagination to be bacl in the high days of magnificence in the Mughal court, and feel the heartbeat of its beautiful and bloody history.

In such circumstances, it is hard to concentrate even at such a bewitching assembly as a mushaira.

This festival of verse is always held at night, and may last until the waking crows and jackdaws disturb the muse as the sky changes through grey pearl to turquoise and then to pale azure with the rising sun.

The audience were seated partly on luxurious oriental carpets, partly on rough cotton durries, and partly on western chairs. The extras, for there always are extras in India, found spaces on the grass or steps or parapets of the formal courts and now dry pools of the old water gardens.

On such an occasion, a university professor may be seated next to the humblest of labourers. We saw just such a juxtapositioning, and it would be hard to say which appreciated the evening more. The labourer was not alone as there were many who had spent the day barefoot, pushing barrows through the streets, and had only the clothes they wore and would sleep under the stars. Others had spent the day in air-conditioned offices, perhaps telephoning the capitals of the world, had wardrobes full of western suits, and would sleep in silken luxury. For the literate and the illiterate, the evening held equal delight because they all loved the language with its wit and flexibility. Delhi has a large Muslim population and many others also speak Urdu.

In front of the former royal apartments, a high platform had been built, backed by a truly regal shamiana screen. It was surrounded by potted plants and covered with white sheeting.

As the poets, all wearing traditional dress, took their places., they removed their shoes and made themselves comfortable on the cushions and bolsters provided. Most of the poets were recognised by the audience and were applauded when they appeared on the platform. Some acknowledged the crowd and others remained aloof. There was a good deal of changing places and shuffling before the programme began, and those familiar with the poets enjoyed watching this positioning and enjoyed the animosities and friendships it indicated.

When the master of ceremonies took the centre of the stage and welcomed the audience, he was applauded, and we all settled down for a long night of verbal dexterity, delicacy and fireworks.

As the hours went by, each poet came forward in turn and recited his work, usually from memory. One or two of the older ones needed help from their notes, but this was viewed sympathetically. The hushed audience were totally involved in the event. During the recitals, a particularly clever couplet, a neat turn of phrase, or a witty juxtaposing of ideas would be applauded, sometimes with the Urdu equivalent of 'bravo', sometimes with a roar of appreciation and even clapping. The poets' eyes twinkled, their chests swelled with pride, or they regarded the audience with a sly expression whilst they produced an even more apt line.

Occasionally, one of the poets waiting in the background would be seen hastily scribbling, perhaps changing a line for a better effect or to secure more praise from the audience than another poet.

The whole event tingled with life and there was plenty of audience participation. Sometimes, and older, well-known poet would be asked to recite a particular popular poem, and those in the audience would hold their breath and glance at each other, waiting for their favourite lines to be spoken. A long sigh and nodding of heads would greet the expected ingenuity, delicacy or pathos.

Eventually, when all the poets had exhausted their store of new poems, and the familiar ones had been recited too, they would be led from the platform by the Master of Ceremonies, heads held high and glancing to neither left nor right, in the knowledge that they had again ensured their places in the hearts of their public, and that their gift, although appreciated by many, was not a commonplace skill.

The audience dispersed, the magic was spirited away, and the raucous vitality of India, like a hot blanket, engulfed us again. Food-sellers cried their wares, beggars accosted us, carts clattered past and stray dogs rummaged through stinking heaps at the roadside.

For one night, the poets had carried us beyond the uncomfortable and the mundane. Those of high estate and those of none, academic and labourer, sharing a delight in the language and imagery of dreams, had met across the gulf which normally separated them. After such an experience, the reality of everyday India becomes once more bearable.

* * * * *

1972 A PASSAGE TO SCOTLAND

Delhi, Jan. 3, 1972

It is rather difficult after these 9 Indian Christmases to imagine an English Christmas Day.

Let me tell you what we got up to.

21st - Chapel carol service was v well attended. We'd decorated it with greenery, and a crib—coffee afterwards for everyone.

23rd - A crowd of 12 college boys ended their round of carol singing round the fire at our house with some lovely carols + grub and coffee and lots of leg-pulling.

24th - Lots of callers. Two very excited little boys. We went to the crib service at St James, Kashmere Gate—A & TP both lit candles.

Aidan could not get to sleep, but at last it was possible to see to the Christmas stockings. We both agreed that they felt exactly right, if one closed one's eyes.

25th - HC in Chapel, and we brought two new university people home for coffee. Then a stream of callers, all very well spaced, fortunately, with some at teatime—a very happy gathering.

26th - To lunch with some friends at the High Commission , but too much booze—everyone but us was boozed up before the end, and we just felt sickened and contaminated. Then we had two tea parties to attend. My hat, by the end of the day I felt like a balloon!

27th - A lovely picnic at Purana Qila with our American friends, the Sheltons. The kids loved it, and so did we. There is a lot of archaeology going on there, with a little museum, so it was interesting as well as enjoyable.

28th - Some friends in for a trolley supper by the fire.

A goes back to school on Thursday.
D is going to the National Archives as often as possible in connection with his research on C.F. Andrews and the book he has been asked to write.
I've packed a couple more boxes.

Delhi, Jan. 31, 1972

A's birthday on the 9th—we had 10 of his 'local' pals, Jagat, Cheti, Anis, Rahis etc to tea −(pakoras and tomato sauce!)

D has his name down with the C of E office for chaplaincies in higher education, but, in strictest confidence, we are under terrific pressure by the Principal-elect, Mr. Rajpal, to return, if only for 2 years, with D as Vice Principal. It is too difficult for us to decide, and we must rely on God to make things clear. We are resisting, now that other arrangements have gone so far and we feel so strongly that at present we are needed in UK *[we were aware that D's sister, Kath, was terminally ill, so that we felt a need to be near her for as long as necessary, and to support D's widowed mother—Kath died within two years of our return]*

We have delayed our departure from here at the Bishop's request, and will arrive in Venice on 2nd or 3rd July, UK about the 4th.

I must say, Janet has been a brick all these years, and wrote such sweet and loving letters during the war. Please tell her to keep on at the cream cakes, though I feel sorry for her and her weight—esp since I am less than 7st 1lb. I expect I shall put a lot on during that Lloyd-Triestino cruise —all that spaghetti, you know.

Delhi, Feb. 15, 1972

We were very heartened to see how helpful & understanding you were about our great problem.

A has started "real maffermatics" at school, but says they're "damn easy".

TP went to the zoo with his school the other day, and was very impressed with an alligator that was lying on the grass. They all took picnics and were treated to ice cream. What a school. All the kids get cuddled. The teachers are so sweet.

Weather here is icy, with heavy snowfalls at Naini Tal and Simla. As I write, I can see one or two ants on the carpet, so it must be going to get warm soon. No doubt, the weather will change in about a week—it is amazing how quickly winter becomes summer.

Delhi, March 26, 1972

TP had a lovely day on the 21st, his birthday—we gave him a swing, which we've fixed on the tree by the front door. Aidan stood him 2 coca colas. He went to school with his 'I'm 4' badge, and was v thrilled to be sung to.

We let A loose with the Arya children at holi.

We went to the British School for a hobbies exhibition the other day, and A got a prize for his Simla pressed-flowers book. He was very pleased.

David Gosling has been staying for a fortnight, and we had visits from Roger Hooker and Dr. Christanand.

I am gathering up clothes for everyone and D has just been given a v nice overcoat by Bob Shelton.

The heat has come with a bang as usual, and left everyone gasping until we get used to it.

Our great news is that we have a prizewinning dog! We took Bhai (official name Snowball) to the Apso dog show at Tibet House, and she won 3rd prize in her class and 1st prize (out of 70) for the best groomed dog. The prize was a Tibetan doc-collar with bells, and a casserole. She loves wearing the bell collar, and has been swanking a lot with everyone who comes to the house. The boys as you can imagine thought it a great day, and I let them collect the prizes.

We're glad we've found her and Catty a good home—with Jyoti Sahi's parents at Dehra Dun.

On Thursday, we had 14 boys from the choir to supper, chiefly to say goodbye to Alexis Gilani, who is going to a tea company in Calcutta—it was a very jolly party.

Y'day, we went out to lunch, and today we went to the High Commission to see a play put on by some of the British School children—it was v good and the boys loved it.

Tim showed David Gosling his toy watch "Yes, its very nice, but it always says the same time" TP "It's the same watch"

Aidan "I know why Adam & Eve weren't allowed to eat that fruit—the snake had been all over it" So much for my Bible teaching!

Delhi, April 1,1972

We had to make our minds up this last 24 hours whether we are to come back here. I can't tell you what prayers and heart-searching and heartache went into it. We can now say that when we arrive in England in July, we shall not return to India ... D has not yet got a job. It is a big relief to know we have made a decision and to feel it is the right one.

A & TP are rather tearful about leaving what is for them home, but I am trying to build up a picture of a happy place in UK.

Delhi, April 7, 1972

[seeking address in S Africa of an old school friend of J's, Chris Skinner, and family, whom we might meet at Durban—but they had moved to Johannesburg]

We will go on the Big Game Reserve tour from Mombasa, and have just made arrangements to meet friends in Cape Town.

I bought a lovely pant suit in Kamla Nagar y'day, and it actually had a label 'Kamla Nagar'—shows how the place has developed of late. I'm buying a few wearable Indian things for myself before we leave.

Delhi, May 1, 1972

You'll never guess what happened! Yes, chicken pox—Aidan is in the throes of it. I only hope TP gets it soon if he is going to, so he is not too spotty to go on board. A has been quite poorly but is now recovering fast.

Before he was ill, he took a bird's nest he had found on the ground for the school nature table, & a lizard's egg I found in my knitting!

I have persuaded the British School to withdraw the Beacon Readers, which have too much violence—that's Parent Power for you!

Today is Mr. Rajpal's first day as Principal. Mr. Sircar has now retired. We had a lovely HC service in Chapel this morning taken by the Bishop and with lots of friends from outside.

I am sitting out in the garden to cool down—the crickets are singing, stars like diamonds in a black velvet sky and the faint scent of jasmine on the occasional breeze.

The boys have been given a baby parrot by a Spanish Jesuit friend! I never thought I cd love such a creature but it is such a pet—even D says it's "a little family pal" It comes when you whistle. We are feeding it with a plastic syringe but are trying to encourage it to peck. It likes to ride on shoulders, mostly T's, but it sat on mine one lunch time, until it decided to try to fly, and landed in the butter dish, much to the boys' delight. It is called Jimmy Green-o. It is now about 3 weeks old, and lives in the nursery.

We've bought a couple of rugs and a lovely table lamp, + spices & various oddments. There are now only a few small items to buy—you know, pearls and diamonds.

Seriously, the packing is 9/10s done. I will close the kitchen on the 20th or 21st, and have college food brought over. Sabra will go and work for the Ghoses—an ideal solution for her.

We'll leave on the 25th for Bombay, and stay at Proctor Road, which is in Byculla, so I'm going to visit the old church there for the sake of my forbears. The boat goes at midnight on the 28th.

We are going out to dinner, a farewell, at Rajpur Road.

Catty and Bhai have gone to their new home—their new owner, Jyoti Sahi's mother, stayed with us last weekend, and I hear the dog has settled marvellously and v much endeared herself to her new mistress at Dehra Dun. Catty has not attempted to run away, but cries a lot. Let's hope he'll settle soon.

Take care. Love. Juliet

* * * * *

[That is Juliet's last surviving letter from our much-loved Indian home. There is one of her letters from the ship, and, fortunately, some of my letters to my mother, covering the time of our journey to Britain, can fill some of the gaps.

As term was over, most of our farewells had been said when we left College on 25th May. We went to chapel, the four of us, for a last service of Holy Communion there, on the morning of our departure. Old Babu Lal and his wife came to the house to say farewell, and we took Sabra and family with us to the station in Aidan's school taxi, driven by Kashmir Singh. At the station quite a crowd had assembled, including the Sircars and the Rajpals, past and future leaders of the College. Prof Faruqi was horrified that we were not travelling air-conditioned, and organised a huge chunk of ice to sit in our compartment until, after about 15 hours, it finally melted—an old-style but effective aid for train-travellers in the heat of late May.

Staying two nights at the Mission Guest House in Bombay, we recalled that we were in Byculla, where Juliet's forbear, Peter Watson, Astronomer, had practised his science some 120 years earlier.

The Lloyd-Triestino ship Asia was bigger than the Caledonia on which we had arrived, though the division into large First Class areas, and the less spacious parts where most of us were, was quite a contrast. The Suez Canal being closed, we took the long route, round southern Africa. We called at Karachi, and at Mombasa, where we had a day-trip to Tsavo National Park, a wonderful experience, especially for the boys. The length of the entire voyage, almost five weeks, was difficult for them to grasp, with their expectation of some magical transfer from Delhi to grandparents in England, but there were lots of children and lots of activities for them on board, not least on the day they got their certificates from 'Neptune' on Crossing the Line. Juliet, ever mindful, had an hour of 'school' prepared for them for each day. At Durban, she and the boys joined a deeply unedifying visit to a display of 'native' culture, leaving me free to spend time with Gandhian friends and contacts at Phoenix Ashram. The majority of passengers, until we reached South Africa, were Indian and the atmosphere was quiet and gracious, but thereafter a large, brash and noisy incursion of Europeans rather drove us into our shells.]

As we reached Tenerife, Juliet wrote a letter to Papa (Mama was on holiday in Morocco)

We've had a marvellous trip from Cape Town and now feel the journey is drawing to a close.

One night, there was an art exhibition on the ship, by the ship's crew. The barman in the lounge is a fantastic artist & had about 10 lovely oils on show. Quite a few good pencil sketches & other bits & pieces by other members of the crew.

The children on board had a v good party the other day, with fabulous presents all round, given out by Father Christmas! Fancy dress was optional, but A dressed as a sort of Batman, & TP was got up as a white horse. During the party, the Captain came round to every table & had a chat with all the kids. The Captain has quite a good life & seems to thoroughly enjoy the dances & mixing with the kids. I can't imagine a British capt being so human.

We arrived here in Tenerife earlier than expected, last night, & so had extra time. We had a very pleasant walk in the town with the boys, & then, after they had gone to bed, D & I had a look in the fabulous shops. The town looked v pretty lit up at night. The view from the ship was almost 'hackneyed', the reflections in the harbour, I mean, so many white & gold wriggly beams from the lights.

This a.m., we were up betimes, & took the boys for another wander round. We bought a very nice little clock for our future sitting-room.

Now, we are bound for Barcelona, arriving Wed.

We get a ship's newspaper every day, & the English weather report is included. I must say, it sounds rather grim

—always ending in rain or cloud. Today, it is cold for us, now that we are away from the land.

Tonight, there is a General Knowledge Quiz, so D & I will have a go.

Our next stop after Barcelona will be Brindisi, then Venice and the train!

Take care.
Love.
Juliet.

P.S. I must say, you are a brick, looking after Nana.

* * * * *

We had left Delhi with absolutely no idea what work we might find in Britain. We took it for granted, as clergy households were still in-clined to do at that time, that whatever turned up for me would be our starting point, and that Juliet would fit in. The London office for chaplaincies in higher education had provided my details to the Bishop of St. Andrews. He was looking for an Anglican Chaplain for the University, and when we reached Cape Town, there had been a letter from him inviting our interest. Scotland! Though we had loved pre-India holidays with relatives on Islay in the Hebrides and our honey-moon in Edinburgh, and Juliet shared her parents' great attachment to that city, the rest of the country, including St. Andrews, seemed almost as exotic a prospect as St. Stephen's College, Delhi, had seemed in the early 1960s. Our sense of vocation, and trust that the right thing would turn up, suggested that, all things being equal, the letter was heaven-sent. Our response was posted from Tenerife, and, to contract this bit of the story, a job and our next home, at Castle Wynd House,

St. Andrews, were agreed within a week of our arrival in Britain, and, soon after, a teaching post turned up for Juliet, with her own craft room at St. Leonard's School.,

Almost imperceptibly (in one sense) Juliet's letter-writing period was over.

~ ~ ~ ~ ~